HOCKEY NIGHT in Canada

BEST OF THE BEST

Ranking the Greatest Players of All Time

SCOTT MORRISON

WITH A FOREWORD BY BOB COLE

CBC

KEY PORTER BOOKS

Library and Archives Canada Cataloguing in Publication

Morrison, Scott
    Hockey Night in Canada's best of the best / Scott Morrison.
ISBN 978-1-55470-316-6
    1. National Hockey League—Biography. 2. National Hockey League—Miscellanea. I. CBC Sports II. Title.
GV847.8.N3M66 2010   796.962092'2   C2010-901883-4

 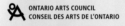

The publisher gratefully acknowledges the support of the Canada Council for the Arts and the Ontario Arts Council for its publishing program. We acknowledge the support of the Government of Ontario through the Ontario Media Development Corporation's Ontario Book Initiative.

We acknowledge the financial support of the Government of Canada through the Canada Book Fund (CBF) for our publishing activities.

Key Porter Books Limited
Six Adelaide Street East, Tenth Floor
Toronto, Ontario
Canada M5C 1H6

www.keyporter.com

www.cbcsports.ca

Text design and electronic formatting: First Image

Mixed Sources
Cert no. SW-COC-001271
© 1996 FSC

Printed and bound in Canada

10 11 12 13 14   5 4 3 2 1

CONTENTS

FOREWORD

In the 40 or so years that I have been calling hockey games, I have had the good fortune of seeing some of the greatest games ever played, in both the National Hockey League and on the international stage.

I started doing hockey on CBC radio in 1969, and I was lucky enough to be doing the play by play in Moscow in 1972 when Paul Henderson scored with only 34 seconds left in that last game as Team Canada won that night 6–5 over the Soviet Union and took the historic Summit Series.

The next year, I joined CBC's *Hockey Night in Canada* on television. Since then I have called too many regular-season games to count, more than 40 Stanley Cup playoffs, All-Star Games, the 1998 Winter Olympics in Nagano, the 2002 Winter Games in Salt Lake City, and the 2006 Games in Turin, Italy.

That gold-medal game in Salt Lake City is one of my favourite memories, with Wayne Gretzky heading up a team that included Mario Lemieux, Joe Sakic, Steve Yzerman, Martin Brodeur, and all the others. It was Canada's first gold medal in 50 years and that was one of the more exciting moments for me.

I've been lucky to have been an eyewitness to hockey history these past four decades and have enjoyed every moment. The Lord willing, I look forward to many more great games in the years to come. I've always felt that we have the greatest sport in the world. The NHL is the best league and the Stanley Cup is and always will be the toughest championship to win.

When I was asked to share my thoughts about which players were the best of the best, I thought it would be an impossible task. How can you come down to just a few names? There have been so many great players: that great gentleman Jean Beliveau; Bobby Orr, with whom I also had the chance to work in the booth years ago; Mr. Hockey, Gordie Howe; the Great One, Wayne Gretzky; magnificent Mario Lemieux; and now, Sidney Crosby.

How can you pick the best with so many to choose from? I do know one thing: thinking of all these players brings back a flood of memories I will cherish forever.

I would like to congratulate Scott Morrison, who joined our CBC's *Hockey Night in Canada* team a few years ago, for putting this terrific book together. I have known Scott throughout my time covering the NHL and I am honoured not only to have been asked by Scott for my opinions, but also to write this foreword in his book.

Enjoy the book and the memories…and the debates that I am sure will ensue.

Bob Cole

Professional sport is all about winning and losing and the desire to be the best. And it is also, at least among fans, often about debate. Which brings us to the premise for this book: determining who are the best hockey players of all-time. Let the debate begin.

Given the insatiable thirst sports fans, especially hockey fans, have for debating which of their favourites players is the best, CBC's *Hockey Night in Canada* decided we would determine the best of the best as *we* saw it.

A few years ago, in HNIC's *By the Numbers* (the first book of this series with Key Porter), we determined the best players of all time by sweater number. This time around, we are doing it by position. And because it is so difficult to compare eras, we have used the 1967 expansion from the Original Six to a dozen teams in the National Hockey League as our great divide.

After all, it is so difficult to compare, say, a Doug Harvey and an Eddie Shore with a Bobby Orr and a Nicklas Lidstrom. All were—and in the case of Lidstrom, still are—great defencemen in their time. But the game was much different when Harvey played than it is now for Lidstrom. So we decided to do pre- and post-expansion assessments, with an overall determination of who were the best general managers and coaches.

In many instances, the number-one player might have been obvious, such as Orr, but numbers 2 through 10 were difficult to determine, with many great players not even cracking the top 10. And not all first choices were obvious. After all, everyone has an opinion of who is number one.

As with HNIC's *By the Numbers*, for this project we put together an esteemed panel from CBC's *Hockey Night in Canada*, with a few interlopers added on to round things out. We had a mix of both young and experienced panelists to make sure we had direction for all the eras. Overall, it is not a precise science, but it was good fun and a challenge for everyone who took part, and ultimately we hope it is provocative and entertaining.

In some cases, certain players played multiple positions, but we tried to focus on the position they played the longest, or at which they had the greatest impact. And we limited the selections to players who participated in the NHL, so some of the Soviet greats and other international stars didn't make the lists. Beyond that, there were no rules.

For each player selected number one at their position, we put together a story detailing career achievements and anecdotes about their careers, special moments, and milestones. For the players selected 2 through 10, we offered shorter biographies, and for all we tried to include something about them you might not have known, or perhaps had forgotten.

It was exciting and thought-provoking to take a stroll down memory lane, in some cases remembering great moments in hockey history and in some cases finding out about some tremendous accomplishments by hockey forefathers.

Hope you enjoy it, too.

Scott Morrison

ACKNOWLEDGEMENTS

Ah, the memories. For a variety of reasons, after writing back-to-back *Hockey Night in Canada* books—*By the Numbers* and *My Greatest Day*—we decided to take last spring off, from publishing, at least. Both books were selling well and my private world had been turned upside down, so we took a break.

Which brings me to the memories of this past spring, what it was like to bring one of these projects together. We were fighting the clock and seemed busier than ever. No sympathy please, but it is no easy feat. And it cannot be done alone. As I have mentioned many times, and it bears repeating, books are born of teamwork and this one wouldn't have made it without the team either.

There are many people to thank and acknowledge for HNIC's *Best of the Best* coming to pass, beginning with the head of CBC Sports Scott Moore and director of production Joel Darling, both of whom have had a profound influence on my career. Both at one time hired me, and both now oversee my work at CBC. Both have also been huge supporters of my work and have found many platforms, including this one, to keep me occupied.

In no particular order, let the thanks begin to everyone important and vital to the cause.

It starts again with HNIC's Anne-Marie Maugeri, who at times seems like my personal assistant in the office, rescuing me with expenses and other nuisances, and putting together the ballots, sending them off to the panel, and then hounding the boys and girls to make sure the ballots were returned promptly.

Thanks, of course, to our cast of voters, who are listed elsewhere in the book, for taking time to pour over the lists and to decide on their best of the best. Once that was done, it came time for the writing, which didn't seem like a big deal when we first sat down to discuss the project, but became decidedly more overwhelming as time marched on. Suddenly, with time flickering, there were a dozen main stories on the number one at each post to be written and nine sidebars in each post—meaning a dozen main stories and 108 sidebars.

There is no way that all gets accomplished without my support group of friends and long-time colleagues who pitched in with research and anecdotes and whatever else they could do to help the project along. So thanks to long-time pals Jim Kelley, Tim Campbell, and Lance Hornby, without whom I would have sunk, not swam. Thanks, too, to colleague Tim Wharnsby for his support and research assistance.

Once all my jottings were done, it was over to the unflappable Andrew Podnieks, my editor again on this book, to pull it all together. Actually, Andrew brought calm to the proceedings very early on when he helped us sort out the many lists and make sure we had everyone in the right position and that all the top 10 lists made sense.

From there it was setting the production schedule and offering support and good words to keep me plowing ahead. Endless thanks again to Andrew, with whom I first worked on *My Greatest Day*. I truly appreciate his professionalism and talents. A distinguished hockey author himself, Andrew was travelling and writing and producing books of his own at the same time as he was doing this.

Then there are the good folks at Key Porter, beginning with Linda Pruessen, who also falls under the categories of professional and talented and unflappable. There are a ton of good people, from publisher Jordan Fenn on down to the designers at First Image, Michael Gray and Rob Scanlan, who have made all three books in this HNIC series look professional and unique. Also, thanks go to the wonderful people at the Hockey Hall of Fame Resource Centre, notably Miragh Bitove, Craig Campbell, and Steve Poirier. As well, to Jason Sundberg at Getty Images for going beyond the call of duty to cull photographs for the book, and to Paul Patskou for his detailed proofreading of the stories and captions.

Finally, a special word of thanks to my son, Mark, who has endured two years no kid should ever have to go through, but who kept me going with his smiles and love.

Scott Morrison

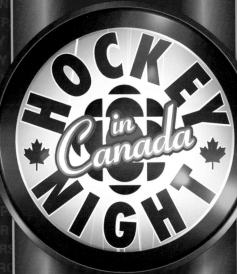

1. JEAN BELIVEAU
2. HOWIE MORENZ
3. HENRI RICHARD
4. DAVE KEON
5. STAN MIKITA
6. TED KENNEDY
7. ALEX DELVECCHIO
8. SYL APPS
9. MILT SCHMIDT
10. SID ABEL

Jean Beliveau

1

In many ways, the nickname said everything about the man himself: "Le Gros Bill"—the big man, the leader, the French folk hero.

That is what Jean Beliveau was for the Montreal Canadiens for many years, during and after his playing career ended. He was regarded by most who watched and especially those who knew him as being a great player, but also a great and classy man.

Beliveau was one of the best, most loved, and most respected Canadiens ever. He scored 507 regular-season goals, which stood for years as a record by a centreman, and added 712 assists. He won the Stanley Cup an amazing 10 times with the Canadiens, including five in a row, and had 79 goals and 97 assists in 162 playoff games. Six times he was a First Team All-Star; four times he was named to the Second Team. He played a total of 1,287 regular-season and playoff games in his 18 full NHL seasons and parts of two others. He won the Hart Trophy, as the league's most valuable player, twice, and the Art Ross Trophy, as the scoring champion, and the Conn Smythe Trophy, as the playoffs' most valuable player, once each.

"We rank him along with Howie Morenz and "Rocket" Richard as one of the all-time greats," legendary Canadiens general manager Sam Pollock once said. "He's one of the top three players ever to put on a Canadiens sweater and certainly rates among the top superstars in the history of the NHL."

At 6'3", 210 lbs., Beliveau was a power forward, bigger than most who skated in that era. But he also played with great skill and grace, though he was also a physical presence when he needed to be. He was often described as being a complete player. He could shoot; he could pass; he could score; and,

when he planted himself in front of the net, he was immovable. It isn't often, either, that one hears the word "elegant" attached to a player's list of epithets, but it applied to Beliveau.

"The two greatest figures of the Canadiens in the past 60 years are "The Rocket" and Jean Beliveau," former Canadiens goaltender Ken Dryden said years ago. "One of them evokes love and the other evokes admiration."

Beliveau was a child prodigy playing in his home town of Victoriaville. Beliveau, whose rights were owned by the Canadiens, played junior hockey in Quebec City, with the Citadelles and Aces, and became a folk hero in that city. He has admitted that he was feted with gifts by local merchants. Whenever he scored three goals he was given suits, shirts, and hats, which he shared with his teammates, and one eatery would give him a free steak dinner for every hat trick. He was even given a car by a local car dealer. He is also the reason Le Colisée was built and was filled every night he played.

While the Canadiens wanted him in Montreal, Beliveau remained loyal to the fans of Quebec City, and after finishing his junior career, he stayed on and played senior hockey with the Aces, who were coached by the legendary "Punch" Imlach. Beliveau was making as much money as many NHLers.

The Canadiens were able to call him up for a maximum of three games a season, but that only whetted their appetite to get him to Montreal full time. There were stories back in the day that the Quebec provincial government warned the Canadiens if they took Beliveau away, they would send a building inspector to check out the Forum, the inference being the Habs wouldn't be pleased

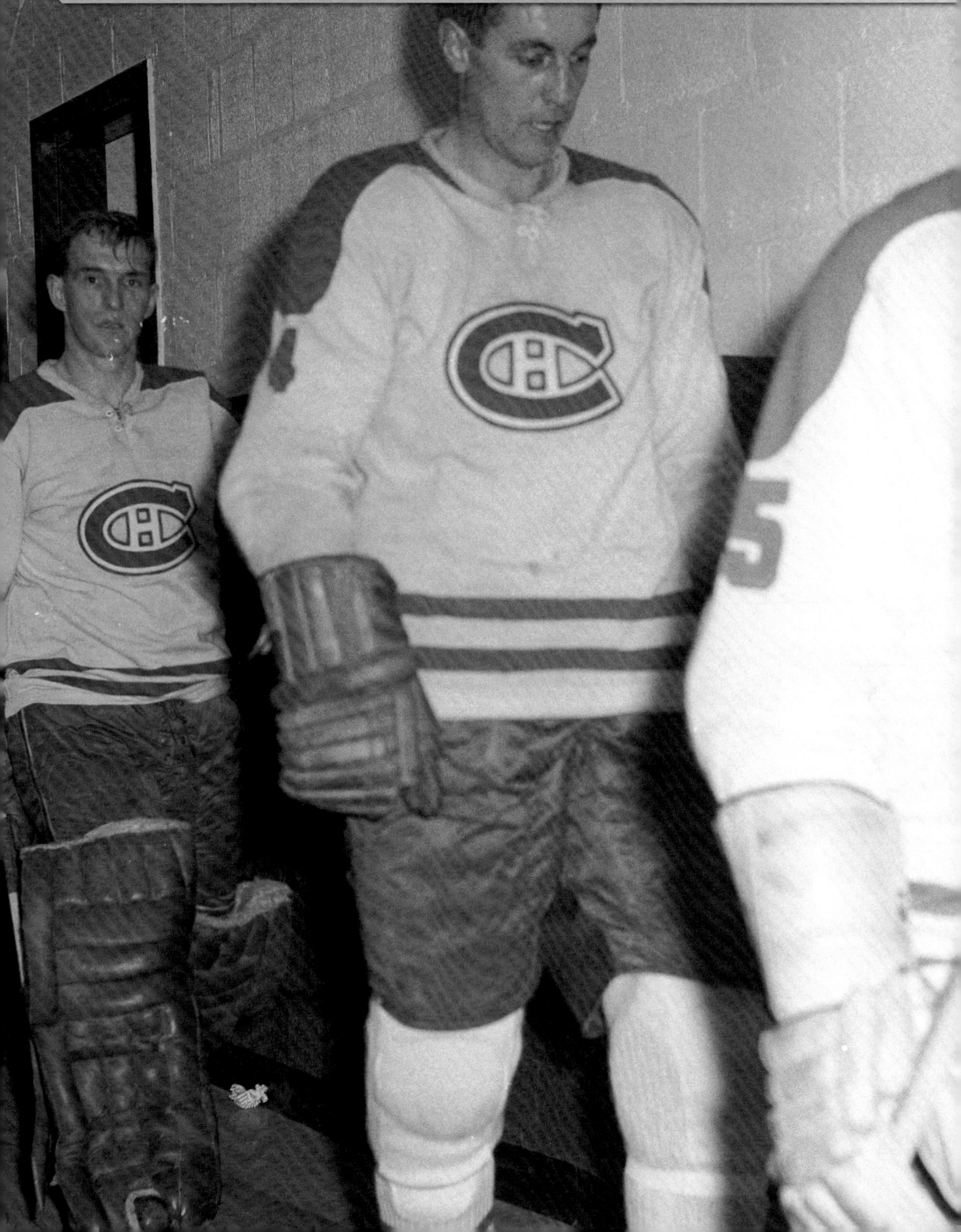

with the expensive upgrades they would be required to make for taking Beliveau from Quebec City.

Eventually, in 1953, the Canadiens were able to get their man, but only after they bought the entire Quebec senior league. Beliveau was signed to a lucrative five-year $100,000 contract to play for the Habs and was given another $10,000 a year for an off-season brewery job. "He was the best thing to come down the pike," Imlach said.

Beliveau suffered an ankle injury in his rookie season and played just 44 games. He began to assert himself physically in his second season, scoring 37 goals, and he increased that total by 10 the following year, while amassing a career-high 143 penalty minutes. That was the season he also won the Hart and Art Ross trophies, was a First Team All-Star, and won the first of the five consecutive Stanley Cup championships.

In 1961, after Doug Harvey was traded, Beliveau was named captain of the Canadiens. He retired as a player after winning his final Stanley Cup in 1971, a few months before his 40th birthday. His name was added to the Stanley Cup another seven times as a club executive, giving him 17 championships in total.

The Canadiens had a Jean Beliveau night in 1971, creating a charitable foundation in his name. He was honoured again with a ceremony in 2003 to celebrate his 50 years with the organization and the team created a trophy in his honour which is awarded annually to the Canadiens player who contributes the most to the community. Beliveau was inducted into the Hockey Hall of Fame in 1972.

"Rarely has the career of an athlete been so exemplary," former Canadian Prime Minister Pierre Elliot Trudeau said of Beliveau. "By his courage, his sense of discipline and honour, his lively intelligence and finesse, his magnificent team spirit, Beliveau has given new prestige to hockey."

↻ Montreal legend Jean Beliveau stations himself in front of the St. Louis goal as the puck trickles towards the goal line.

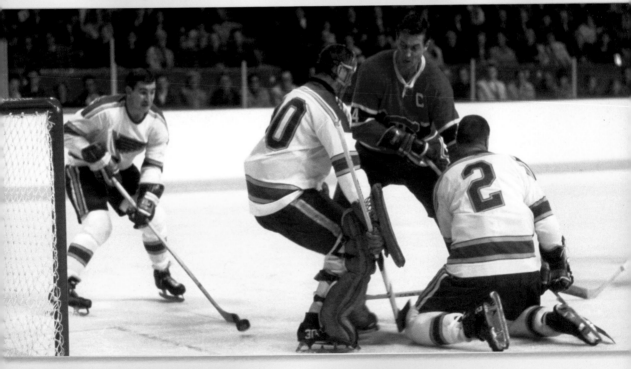

Bet you didn't know

One of classiest people to play the game, Beliveau was the ultimate gentleman off the ice as well. Legendary Montreal sportswriter Red Fisher told the story of Beliveau being approached in a corner store by a woman looking for an autograph. It was obvious the woman recognized Beliveau, but wasn't entirely certain who he was. But she asked for the autograph for her son and Beliveau signed it.

"You play for the Alouettes [Montreal's football team], don't you?" the woman asked.

"Yes, I do," said Beliveau, who would not embarrass the woman.

Beliveau was a stickler with signing his autograph, always making sure the signature was legible, always being patient and accommodating with the fans. "When a youngster asks me for my autograph, I always take the time to give a good signature," Beliveau once said. "I always tell the rookies that if you're going to take the time to give an autograph, make sure that the youngster can read your name."

Beliveau's grace and dignity caught the eyes of politicians, too. Former Canadian Prime Minister Jean Chretien offered Beliveau the post of Governor General in 1994, but he declined for family reasons. He was also offered a seat in the Canadian Senate.

↻ Beliveau (right) fights for the puck along the boards.

Howie Morenz

The "Mitchell Meteor," as he was first known—for his birthplace and great speed—was voted the Montreal Canadiens' greatest player of the first half of the century. Howie Morenz won the Stanley Cup in his first season in Montreal and two more with the Canadiens before he departed for Chicago, though he was later re-acquired by the team most associated with his life and career. He won the Hart Trophy, as most valuable player, three times and was regarded as being arguably the first true superstar in the NHL.

Morenz scored 271 goals in 14 seasons. According to hockey analyst and historian, Dick Irvin, "they called Howie Morenz the Babe Ruth of hockey. He was the guy who the people paid to see, on both sides of the border, especially in the United States, so he was quite an influence on the game that way."

When he changed hometowns his nickname changed to the "Stratford Streak." Sadly, Morenz died at the young age of 34 from a blood clot. Just a few weeks earlier he had broken his leg in a game against Chicago. His funeral, on March 11, 1937, attracted thousands of mourners to the Forum to honour Morenz.

He was one of the first inductees into the Hockey Hall of Fame in 1945.

Bet you didn't know

The Morenz legacy carries on in the NHL to this day. Morenz's daughter, Marlene, married Montreal Canadiens star Bernie "Boom Boom" Geoffrion, whose number 5 was retired by the Canadiens on March 11, 2006 (the same day of Morenz's funeral, 69 years later). During the ceremony, as Geoffrion's number was raised to the rafters of the Bell Centre, Morenz's number 7 was lowered to meet it.

Geoffrion's son Danny played parts of three seasons in the NHL and now his son, Blake, who is Morenz's great grandson, signed an entry-level contract with the Nashville Predators in 2010, making it four generations of the family to play in the NHL.

Henri Richard

He may not be the most famous of the Richard brothers—overshadowed for a time in his career by his brother Maurice, "The Rocket"—but Henri Richard was a great hockey player in his own right. And he was a winner.

Indeed, Richard, who was known as the "Pocket Rocket," won the Stanley Cup a record 11 times—including five in his first five seasons in the league—and played in a dozen Finals. He also shares the record, with Red Kelly, for playing in the most (65) Stanley Cup Final games, in which he registered 47 points. He was a First Team All-Star once, when he led the league with 52 assists, and was three times named to the Second Team.

In his 1,256 regular-season games, Richard scored 358 goals and had 1,046 points, at the time the ninth player to surpass 1,000 points. He was not as big or as tough as his brother, at 5'7", 160 pounds. But Henri was an elegant skater, a terrific playmaker, and a gifted goal scorer. He was also a relentless checker, good at both ends of the rink.

And he was a winner, part of those great Canadiens teams that won the Cup seemingly every year. He was inducted into the Hockey Hall of Fame in 1979.

Bet you didn't know

Henri Richard played a total of 20 seasons in the NHL, but won a Stanley Cup in more than half, an incredible 11 times. He retired in 1975, just before the Canadiens went on a run of four more Stanley Cup wins.

Just twice during his career did Richard miss the playoffs—once because of injury, and once because the Habs were eliminated on the final day of the season.

Dave Keon

He is considered by many long-time Toronto Maple Leafs watchers as the best two-way player in the team's history. Dave Keon might have been one of their best players, period. And certainly one of the most popular Leafs ever.

Keon, who joined the Leafs in 1960 after a successful junior career at St. Michael's College, one of Toronto's sponsored clubs, was a great playmaker and goal scorer, and most often he had his offensive success while playing against the opposition's top line. Indeed, he was a brilliant two-way player.

That first season with the Leafs, Keon scored 20 goals and had 45 points to earn the Calder Trophy as top rookie in the league. He scored 20 or more goals for five more consecutive seasons and 11 times in total with the Leafs. Three times he led the club in scoring and twice won the Lady Byng Trophy, which is given to the player who combines sportsmanship and gentlemanly play with a high standard of play. In both of those seasons he had just two penalty minutes all season.

Keon, who was also a top penalty killer, set a league record in 1971 with eight shorthanded goals. He was also regarded for having a wicked backhand shot, arguably the best in the league, and at times even used a backhand slap shot. He finished his NHL career with 396 goals and 986 points in 18 seasons, with just 117 penalty minutes. The most he had in any one season was a meagre 26.

Keon won the Stanley Cup four times with the Leafs, including their final time in 1967 when he won the Conn Smythe Trophy as the most valuable player in the playoffs. He was captain of the Leafs for six seasons and was inducted into the Hockey Hall of Fame in 1986.

Bet you didn't know

Like a lot of Maple Leafs to follow him, Dave Keon's departure from the club after 15 seasons was not a pleasant one. He was involved in a messy battle with outspoken club owner Harold Ballard, who had previously signed his star centre to the richest contract in club history, but when it expired in 1975 Ballard publicly questioned his leadership.

Keon departed for the World Hockey Association, where he played for four seasons with Minnesota, Indianapolis, and New England, before returning to the NHL with the Hartford Whalers. With the legendary Gordie Howe as a teammate, Keon played in Hartford for the final three seasons of his career.

He remained estranged from the Leafs organization even after Ballard died, unimpressed with how the club honoured its former stars, although he finally did return for a club celebration of the 1967 championship team in 2007. His cousin was Tod Sloan, a star with Leafs teams from an earlier era.

Stan Mikita

For years early in his career Stan Mikita was, as former coach and analyst Harry Neale put it, "a miserable son of a gun on the ice." But he went from being one of the nastiest to one of the most gentlemanly players on the ice. It was quite the transformation, but any way he played Mikita was a star player.

"He got a lot of penalties," said Neale. "His young daughter got mad when she saw her dad going to the penalty box so often and so he just reversed his form, not on talent, just all of a sudden he was a candidate for the Lady Byng Trophy. It was an amazing turnaround because he had a dirty streak when he started. He was a really skilled player and one of those guys who hung on to the puck until the last second and made the good play."

Mikita was also a good stickhandler and a terrific offensive player. Playing on the "Scooter Line" with Ken Wharram and Ab McDonald (and later Doug Mohns), he won the Art Ross Trophy as NHL scoring leader four times, one of those times leading the league with 97 points. He won the Hart Trophy as most valuable player twice and, yes, after transforming his game he won the Lady Byng Trophy twice.

Mikita also won a Stanley Cup with the Black Hawks in 1961, which was his second full season in Chicago. That was the last Stanley Cup the team won until the spring of 2010.

Born in Czechoslovakia, "Stosh" as he was known to his teammates, came to Canada when he was eight and had a terrific junior career with the St. Catharines Teepees, leading the OHA in points his final season. During those early seasons in which he spent considerable time in the penalty box, Mikita had four times in six years more than 100 penalty minutes. But after the penalties stopped, the points didn't and his game was every bit as good, if not better.

In fact, in 1967 and 1968, Mikita won the Ross, Byng, and Hart Trophies. He was a First Team All-Star six times and a Second Team All-Star twice in his 22 seasons, finishing with 541 goals (which included 14 straight 20-plus goal seasons) and 1,467 points before retiring in 1980. He was inducted into the Hockey Hall of Fame in 1983.

Bet you didn't know

Stan Mikita gained more than his fair share of glory during his playing career, but he gained a different kind of notice after his career was over. In the movie *Wayne's World*, starring Canadian actor and hockey fan Mike Myers, the doughnut shop was called Stan Mikita's, which was a take-off of the famous Tim Hortons doughnut–coffee shop chain.

Ted Kennedy

Ted Kennedy was a fierce competitor and was regarded as one of the top faceoff men of his day. Kennedy, who joined the Leafs in 1943, helped to lead the team to five Stanley Cup wins in a seven-year span, including three in a row. Three times he was a Second Team All-Star, and he won the Hart Trophy as the league's most valuable player in 1955. He retired after that season, though he returned a couple of years later for a 30-game stint with the Leafs.

Kennedy played on a line with Howie Meeker and Vic Lynn, which was originally known as "The Kid Line II" and later called the "KLM Line." Kennedy was named captain of the Leafs in 1948, succeeding Syl Apps. He was also highly regarded for his determined play—so much so that club management created an award in 1953, the J.P. Bickell Trophy, which was given to the most valuable Leaf. Kennedy won it that first year and two seasons later.

A fan favourite during his 13 seasons with the Leafs, there was one fan in particular, John Arnott, would often holler from the stands, "Come on, Teeder!" when the Leafs were behind in a game.

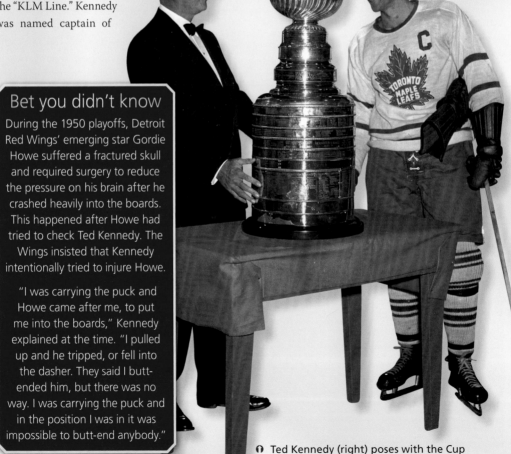

Bet you didn't know

During the 1950 playoffs, Detroit Red Wings' emerging star Gordie Howe suffered a fractured skull and required surgery to reduce the pressure on his brain after he crashed heavily into the boards. This happened after Howe had tried to check Ted Kennedy. The Wings insisted that Kennedy intentionally tried to injure Howe.

"I was carrying the puck and Howe came after me, to put me into the boards," Kennedy explained at the time. "I pulled up and he tripped, or fell into the dasher. They said I butt-ended him, but there was no way. I was carrying the puck and in the position I was in it was impossible to butt-end anybody."

⋔ Ted Kennedy (right) poses with the Cup alongside Premier Leslie Frost.

7

Alex Delvecchio

Alex Delvecchio enjoyed success quickly in his NHL career with the Detroit Red Wings. In his rookie season, he showed poise beyond his years and helped lead the Red Wings to a Stanley Cup win in 1952.

The following season he took over from the legendary Sid Abel at centre between Gordie Howe and Ted Lindsay on the famed "Production Line." That same season he was named a Second-Team All-Star for the first of two times during his 24 seasons with the Red Wings. Detroit went on to win the Stanley Cup the following two seasons.

Delvecchio was a skilled and gentlemanly player on the ice, three times winning the Lady Byng Trophy. He scored 20 goals or more a dozen times and was part of another terrific line for a couple of seasons in the late '60s with Howe on his right wing and Frank Mahovlich on the left. During the 1968–69 season that line scored a then-record 118 goals.

Delvecchio finished his distinguished career with 456 goals and 1,281 regular-season points, with another 35 goals and 104 points in the playoffs. After retiring, he had a couple of stints as coach

of the Red Wings and was also general manager before being dismissed in 1977, the same year he was inducted into the Hockey Hall of Fame.

Bet you didn't know

For most people the nickname "Fats" wouldn't normally be a term of endearment. But it was for Alex Delvecchio. That was the name his Detroit Red Wings teammates gave him, not because he had weight issues, but rather because he had a usually happy, cherubic face. Delvecchio was one of the more popular Red Wings and had his sweater number 10 raised to the rafters at Joe Louis Arena on November 10, 1991.

Syl Apps

Syl Apps was admired as much as a man as he was a hockey player. He was a hugely skilled centre who won the Calder Trophy in 1937 and registered 20 or more goals five times in his 10-year career with the Toronto Maple Leafs. Although he was big and strong and tough, Apps was also disciplined and was awarded the Lady Byng Trophy in 1942, playing 38 regular-season games and not incurring a single penalty. He earned just two minutes in 13 memorable playoff games.

The 1942 Stanley Cup Final, of course, was one for the ages, as the Maple Leafs lost the first three games to the Detroit Red Wings but battled back to win the series in seven games. It was the only time it happened until 1975, when the New York Islanders did the same to the Pittsburgh Penguins and 2010 when the Philadelphia Flyers rebounded against the Boston Bruins. To this day, though, the Leafs are still the only team to make such an historic rally in the Cup Final.

Apps, who was twice a First Team All-Star and three times was named to the Second Team, helped lead the Leafs to three Stanley Cup titles, the other two in 1947 and 1948. He was a gifted, all-round athlete. He was first spotted by the Leafs while playing football at McMaster University in Hamilton, Ontario. He was also a pole vaulter and competed for Canada in the 1936 Berlin Olympics, where he finished sixth in that discipline. Apps joined the Leafs for the 1936–37 season.

He was inducted into the Hockey Hall of Fame in 1961 and is also a member of Canada's Sports Hall of Fame and the Canadian Amateur Athletics Hall of Fame. His number 10 was honoured with a banner by the Leafs.

Bet you didn't know

According to the Hockey Hall of Fame archives, during the 1942–43 season Syl Apps crashed into a goalpost and broke his leg. He played just 29 games that season. As the story goes, Apps, who was making $6,000 a season, approached Maple Leafs' owner Conn Smythe with a cheque for $1,000.

"He said 'Conn, I'm making more than I deserve. I want to give you this cheque,'" Smythe related. "Well, I almost died of heart failure. Of course, I refused his cheque. I felt that anyone who thought in such terms was bound to square off what he thought was a debt the following season."

Actually, the following season Apps left the Leafs to join the Canadian Army and serve in the Second World War. He returned in 1945 to play three more seasons before retiring at age 33.

Milt Schmidt

As a 17-year-old on a tryout with the Boston Bruins, Milt Schmidt impressed coach Art Ross so much that he was offered a contract. But he turned it down because it wasn't enough money. Schmidt eventually signed with the Bruins a short while later in the fall of 1936 and went on to a terrific career, playing on the famed "Kraut Line" with childhood friends from Kitchener, Ontario, Woody Dumart and Bobby Bauer. In the 1939–40 season, that line finished 1-2-3 in league scoring, the first time that had ever happened.

Schmidt won the Stanley Cup twice, in 1939 and 1941 with the Bruins, and led the league in scoring in 1940. He also won the Hart Trophy in 1951.

A gifted playmaker, Schmidt never feared trying to beat defencemen along the boards and was punished physically for his efforts. Bad knees forced Schmidt, who had missed three seasons midway through his career to serve with the air force in the Second World War, to retire part way through the 1954–55 season. He had 229 goals and 575 points which, at the time, put him third in the NHL in career points.

After retiring, Schmidt went on to coach and manage the Bruins and later was general manager of the Washington Capitals. He was inducted into the Hockey Hall of Fame in 1961.

Bet you didn't know

Milt Schmidt's sweater number 15 was retired by the Boston Bruins on March 13, 1980, and raised to the rafters at the old Boston Garden. But it almost came down.

According to Schmidt, former Bruins general manager Harry Sinden once asked if he could take it down and put the number 15 back into circulation.

"He said the numbers were getting so high they were looking like a football team," said Schmidt. "I said, 'Hey, if you want to do it, what can I do? Maybe there would be some criticism, but it's up to you.'"

The number 15 remains retired and in the rafters in Boston.

Sid Abel

For years Sid Abel was the centre on one of the most famous lines in hockey—"The Production Line"—with Gordie Howe on the right wing and Ted Lindsay on the left.

The line was first put together during the 1946–47 season with excellent results, but they really found their stride and their nickname during the 1948–49 season, during which Abel led the Red Wings in scoring with 28 goals and 54 points and won the Hart Trophy. The following season he had a career best 34 goals and 69 points and 61 points the season after that.

Like a lot of players in his day, Abel left the team for two years because of the Second World War. He was twice named to both the First and Second All-Star teams and won the Stanley Cup three times with the Red Wings—1943, 1950, and 1952.

It was after that final Stanley Cup that the Red Wings, figuring that Abel's best days were behind him, traded him to the Chicago Black Hawks. It wasn't a popular move, but it was probably a good hockey one. While with the Black Hawks for two seasons, Abel served as a player and coach. He retired after that brief stint in Chicago and returned to Detroit as a colour commentator for their televised games. He eventually became coach, replacing an ill Jimmy Skinner during the 1957–58 season. As a coach, Abel led the Red Wings to the Stanley Cup Final four times, but each time they lost, first to Chicago, then twice to Toronto, and, finally, to Montreal.

Abel also served as general manager in Detroit, then later with the St. Louis Blues and Kansas City Scouts. He finishes his career with 189 goals and 472 points over 14 seasons and was inducted into the Hockey Hall of Fame in 1969. He had his number 12 retired by the Red Wings in 1995.

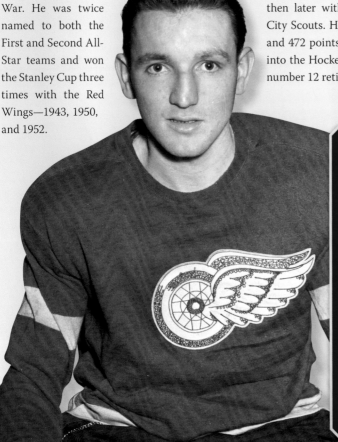

Bet you didn't know

Sid Abel had a nickname you wouldn't soon forget. And he would never forget how he got it. He was known to his teammates as "Boot Nose." According to reports of the day, he acquired that not-so-flattering handle after he had his nose severely broken in a fight with Montreal Canadiens star Maurice "Rocket" Richard. It seems that Abel was jawing with Richard, leveled a few wisecracks and insults, and was ultimately greeted with a rather vicious punch to the nose. He was "Boot Nose" ever after.

MODERN ERA
CENTRE

1. Wayne Gretzky
2. Mario Lemieux
3. Steve Yzerman
4. Mark Messier
5. Joe Sakic
6. Bryan Trottier
7. Phil Esposito
8. Bobby Clarke
9. Sidney Crosby
10. Peter Forsberg

Wayne Gretzky

What the legendary Bobby Orr was to the game in the 1970s, Wayne Gretzky was in the 1980s and '90s. Let the debate rage on who was the greatest player ever.

Like Orr before him, Gretzky dominated the league for most of the two decades in which he played. He rewrote the record book, at one time holding or sharing an incredible 61 NHL records, which was a record of its own. When it came to scoring and point production Gretzky did it all and in a huge way.

He still holds the league single-season records for most goals (92), assists (163), and points (215, which came four years after earning 212). Four times he had more than 200 points, the only player to surpass the 200-mark even once. Not surprisingly, he also holds most career scoring records: goals (894), assists (1,963), and points (2,857).

He was also the fastest ever to score 50 goals in a season, accomplishing it in a remarkable 39 games. Five of those 50, by the way, came in the 39th game.

It is safe to say many of Gretzky's scoring records may never be broken, or certainly no time soon. Put it this way: Gretzky has more career assists than the second leading scorer of all-time—his childhood idol, Gordie Howe—has points (1,850).

Gretzky was a superstar virtually from the time he first started playing on the backyard rink his father, Walter, built at their home in Brantford, Ontario. Gretzky was a kid phenom at every level of minor and junior hockey, eventually turning pro in the WHA in 1978 with the Indianapolis Racers, a team that folded early in the '78– '79 season and sold him to the Edmonton Oilers.

He came to the NHL with the Oilers in 1979 when the two leagues merged. During his nine seasons with the Oilers, he helped lead them to four Stanley Cup championships in five years. He was traded in 1988 by owner Peter Pocklington, who had signed an 18-year-old Gretzky to a 21-year personal services contract. Gretzky was dealt along with Mike Krushelnyski and Marty McSorley to the Los Angeles Kings and owner Bruce McNall for $15 million, Jimmy Carson, Martin Gelinas, and three first-round draft picks. That trade prompted the phrase that still lives on: "If Gretzky can be traded, anyone can be traded."

"The Great One," as he was called, helped put hockey on the map in Southern California. The Kings became wildly successful at the box office and ultimately on the ice, where they advanced to the Stanley Cup Final in 1993 only to lose in five games to the Montreal Canadiens.

Gretzky later played part of a season with the St. Louis Blues in 1996 before signing with the New York Rangers and ending his career on Broadway, playing his final game at age 38 on April 18, 1999, at Madison Square Garden.

Once deemed too small and too slow to star in professional hockey, Gretzky had surprising speed, an incredible vision of the ice, wonderful playmaking skills, and a deceptively good shot. In short, he could do it all. He could dominate and control games with his masterful puckhandling skills. Often he would set up behind the opposition's goal, an area which eventually became known as his "office," and set up the attack.

He had an incredible sense of knowing where the puck would go next. His passing ability was truly remarkable. He would lead rushes up the ice and either hit a breaking winger with a pass, or stop and curl inside the blue line, then make his play to the trailing man, the first player to use the last man coming forward.

Gretzky won the Hart Trophy nine times overall and in eight consecutive seasons. He won the Art Ross Trophy as scoring champion 10 times, including seven straight years. He also won the Conn Smythe in two of the Oilers' four championship seasons, the Lady Byng five times, and the Pearson five times. He was the NHL's plus-minus leader four times.

Gretzky also had great success on the international stage, playing in World Junior and World Championships, an Olympics in 1998, and leading Team Canada to victory in the 1984, 1987, and 1991 Canada Cup tournaments. That 1987 tournament was especially memorable because of the three-game finals with the Soviet Union, a series that produced arguably the greatest hockey ever.

Canada lost the first game, 6–5, in Montreal. Two nights later, in Hamilton, with the team's back against the wall, Gretzky played "the greatest game I ever played in my life." He had five assists that night,

including one on Mario Lemieux's double overtime goal, which gave Canada a 6–5 win to force a memorable third game, in which Canada overcame a three-goal deficit to win again, 6–5, with Gretzky setting up Lemieux for the winning goal with just 1:26 left in the game.

"That series was probably the best hockey I've ever played," said Gretzky. Indeed, there was no shortage of great games in his incredible career. Gretzky was inducted into the Hockey Hall of Fame immediately after he retired, just the 10th player to skip the mandatory three-year wait. The Hall announced that he was to be the last so honoured.

After retiring, Gretzky became general manager for Team Canada in the 2002 Olympics, in which they won gold for the first time in 50 years. He went on to coach the Phoenix Coyotes for a few seasons before stepping down in the fall of 2009 when the franchise was in financial distress.

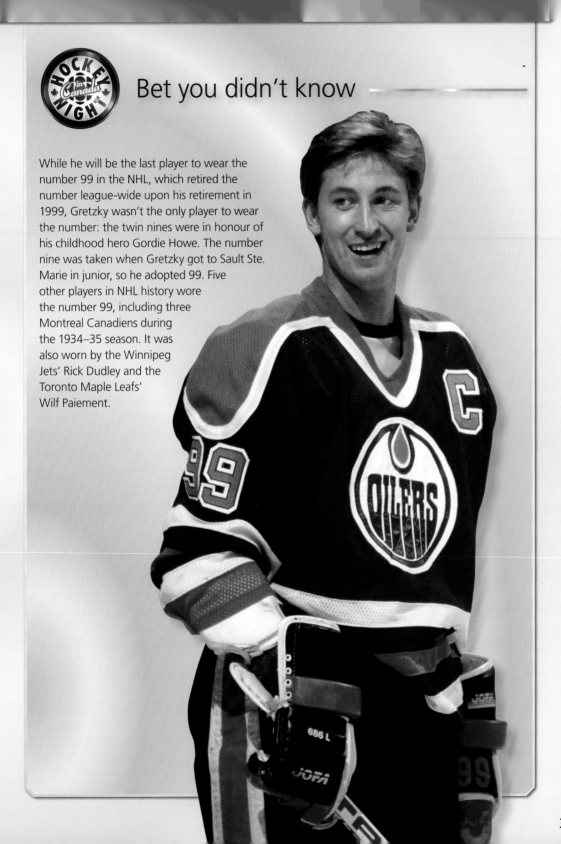

Bet you didn't know

While he will be the last player to wear the number 99 in the NHL, which retired the number league-wide upon his retirement in 1999, Gretzky wasn't the only player to wear the number: the twin nines were in honour of his childhood hero Gordie Howe. The number nine was taken when Gretzky got to Sault Ste. Marie in junior, so he adopted 99. Five other players in NHL history wore the number 99, including three Montreal Canadiens during the 1934–35 season. It was also worn by the Winnipeg Jets' Rick Dudley and the Toronto Maple Leafs' Wilf Paiement.

Mario Lemieux

Few pro-hockey players have come back from as many hard knocks as Mario Lemieux. He struggled at the 1984 Memorial Cup and there were questions about his passion to play in Pittsburgh early on, as well as doubts about his leadership and his commitment to play for his country. Ultimately, though, his desire could never be questioned.

His troubles from spinal disc herniation, chronic hip tendinitis, severe back pain, and, most serious of all, non-Hodgkins lymphoma, seemed to point to a pre-mature end to his career. But Lemieux proved his mettle, determination, and will through multiple Stanley Cups, Canada Cups, and days when it hurt to get out or bed or tie his own skates.

It was impossible not to cheer when he flew to Philadelphia on the last day of his radiation treatment in 1993 and later came out of retirement to play on December 27, 2000. In front of a huge TV audience he emerged from almost three years of retirement. His number 66 banner was lowered from the rafters and put back into storage as he had an assist 33 seconds into the game against Toronto.

He ended with 1,723 regular-season points in just over 900 games. Contemporaries such as Wayne Gretzky and Bobby Orr wondered how much more damage he would have done to the record book had he not been troubled by so many health issues. But Lemieux's work in Pittsburgh wasn't done after he retired for good in 2006. Having joined ownership to keep the team in town and protect his own club investment, he stayed to ensure the long-term viability of the franchise and a transition to a new arena.

Lemieux somehow managed, through all the ailments and injury, to finish with 690 goals and 1,723 points. He won the Art Ross Trophy six times and was awarded the Hart Trophy three times, twice leading the Penguins to Cup wins. He scored the winning goal in the 1987 Canada Cup and captained the gold-medal venture for Canada at the 2002 Olympics.

Bet you didn't know

Mario Lemieux and goaltender Patrick Roy were born on the same day, October 5, 1965, in the province of Quebec. In the 1990s, the two Hall of Famers were part of four combined Stanley Cups in Montreal, Pittsburgh, and Colorado. As a kid, Lemieux and his young hockey-playing brothers would often try to bring snow inside the house to replicate ice when it was too dark outside.

Steve Yzerman

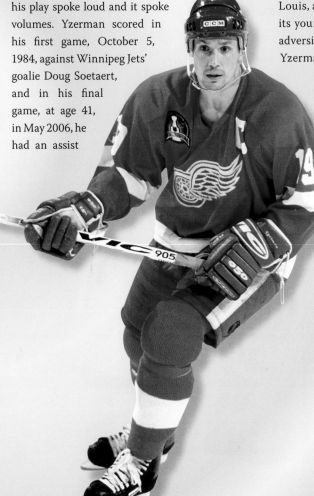

Red and white have done well by Steve Yzerman, and vice-versa. Whether it was turning around Detroit's fortunes (and captaining it to three Stanley Cups), playing for Team Canada, or pushing the national squad's buttons from the executive office, Yzerman had the gift to turn red and white into Olympic gold and sterling Stanley silver.

When seeking the right player to rebuild their crumbling Original Six team in the early 1980s, the Wings went with a baby-faced teen from the Peterborough Petes who spoke barely above a whisper in public. But on the ice, his play spoke loud and it spoke volumes. Yzerman scored in his first game, October 5, 1984, against Winnipeg Jets' goalie Doug Soetaert, and in his final game, at age 41, in May 2006, he had an assist on a Robert Lang goal in a playoff game against Edmonton.

In between came the triple Cups, his Lester B. Pearson Award in 1989 as the players' choice for MVP, the Conn Smythe Trophy for the Wings' 1998 Cup (at present the last team to repeat as champions), the Selke Trophy, Bill Masterton Trophy, and 10 All-Star Game nods.

But it wasn't all roses and sunshine. The Wings were turned back several times in the early 1990s trying to get past powerful Western Conference opponents Edmonton, Calgary, St. Louis, and Chicago. It took a toll on the team and its young captain. "I was able to deal with some adversity, come out of it, and be a better player," Yzerman said.

Bitten by the management bug after retirement, Yzerman joined the Wings' front office, graduated to executive director of Team Canada, and following the 2010 gold-medal run at the Olympics, took his first NHL general manager's post with Tampa Bay.

Bet you didn't know

NHL history would have been different had the 1983 draft order been slightly altered. Picking fourth, Detroit had an excellent American centre in mind, Pat LaFontaine, but the New York Islanders grabbed him at number three. Still available were Cam Neely, Russ Courtnall, Claude Lemieux, and Peter Zezel, all tempting players. But GM Jim Devellano went with Yzerman. "As best as you can know an 18-year-old, we felt we had found our cornerstone," Devellano said.

Mark Messier

If there were a Mount Rushmore of NHL players, jut-jawed Mark Messier would have a place of prominence on it. The image of Messier staring down a rival forward, the officials, or a member of the media is still vivid many years after retirement and his election to the Hall of Fame.

If the sight of Wayne Gretzky, Jari Kurri, and Paul Coffey in full flight was the beauty of the Edmonton Oilers, Messier could be its dark side. During an early 1980s series against the Montreal Canadiens, Messier made some menacing gestures toward Habs' great Larry Robinson, which the former deemed "politically incorrect" but necessary to demonstrate that the upstart Oilers were not afraid.

Messier was not shy about asserting himself on the ice or in the dressing room. When not abetting Gretzky (four of his five 100-point seasons came with the Oilers prior to the Great One's departure), Messier could spark the team on his own, implementing a shooting tip from coach Glen Sather early in his career to take more wrist shots than unpredictable slaps, making himself even more dangerous.

Messier lasted longer than any of the dynasty-era Oilers, playing 25 years and a record 1,992 regular-season and playoff games. After winning Edmonton's fifth Cup with Gretzky gone, he took his act to Broadway where he became the first Rangers captain to win a Cup there in 54 years.

He stretched his career over four decades, having started in 1979, ending in 2004 and wrapping up as the last WHA player to have moved to the NHL and the last NHLer to have played in the 1970s.

Bet you didn't know

Mark Messier's famous speech "guaranteeing" the Rangers would come back and beat the New Jersey Devils en route to winning the 1994 Cup wasn't supposed to get out of the New York dressing room. "He'd actually just said it to me and a couple of people around him," teammate Joey Kocur said. "It wasn't supposed to get out in the press and, when it did, it took on a life of its own. But it was the kind of thing that leaders and superstars do. He had a hat trick in the game."

Joe Sakic

Joe Sakic is regarded as a quiet man, due in part to being raised in a Croatian-speaking household where he didn't master English until past his kindergarten years. He was also deeply affected by events in December 1986, when the bus carrying his Swift Current Broncos WHL team crashed on a wintry highway, killing four teammates.

Nor did Sakic ever seem to get a lot of fanfare for his on-ice exploits, perhaps because he played for much of his career out of sight of the eastern media in Denver. But when he finally stepped aside after 20 years, he was sitting in the top 10 of NHL scoring, with 1,641 regular-season points, two Stanley Cups, and a wagon train of other awards. Those numbers speak volumes about his accomplishments as one of the best centres in the game's history.

Sakic had almost 300 points in his last two years of junior, electing to play in Swift Current his last year of eligibility in 1987–88 despite most scouts insisting he was ready for the NHL and the Quebec Nordiques. The team had two first round picks in '87, starting with defenceman Bryan Fogarty. In all, nine picks who would have very limited NHL success came and went before the Nords got Sakic at 15th.

Reinforced by the players acquired in the Eric Lindros trade, Sakic and the Nords went to Denver with the change of ownership and won the '96 Cup, repeating the feat five years later with Ray Bourque added to that team. Sakic handed the Cup to Bourque the moment it was presented, a memorable gesture in the annals of Stanley Cup history.

Sakic also won the Hart Trophy in 2001, joining Bobby Clarke, Wayne Gretzky, and Mark Messier as the only men to be captain of a Cup winner and be named MVP the same season.

Bet you didn't know

After spending his first year off to coach his son and that of Avs' coach Joe Sacco in a Denver-area minor hockey league, Sakic is interested in getting into management. Talks were planned with the Colorado front office for the summer of 2010. Sakic's record of eight playoff overtime goals is still safe a year after he departed the game. His extra-time goals are spread over six springs and are two more than second-place Maurice Richard.

Bryan Trottier

As a kid playing minor hockey, Bryan Trottier was once asked to play defence, a concept so disagreeable that he refused to chase his man into the corner or protect the net. Instead, he set up in front at the other end, oblivious to his father's shouts.

Once a scorer, always a scorer, and Trottier certainly did his share of putting the puck in the net.

Though the Saskatchewan-born centre won only one Art Ross Trophy, in 1978–79—a fellow named Gretzky came along next year and made Trottier's string of 100-point seasons look routine—he compiled more than 1,600 regular-season and playoff points.

Trottier also finished with more Stanley Cups than Gretzky as a player (6–4), starting with four straight as a New York Islanders forward and two more with Pittsburgh. Centring the Isles' potent "Trio Grande" line with Mike Bossy and Clark Gillies, Trottier could seemingly do no wrong. However, he made some off-ice decisions that tested the patience of many, such as preferring to play for the United States at the 1984 Canada Cup and taking a head coaching job with the Isles' most bitter rivals, the New York Rangers. Much later, he became an assistant coach with the Colorado Avalanche and earned one more Cup. But time healed the wounds and Trottier returned to the Island as executive director of player development, holding the post until 2010.

Bet you didn't know

Trottier sits 15th in NHL career points, but played the third-fewest regular-season games (1,279) of anyone above him on that list. He claims never to have suffered an injury that kept him out more than a week, the exception being a broken jaw from a wild cross-ice Denis Potvin pass. The fluke injury occurred late in the season and healed during the summer.

Phil Esposito

Phil Esposito is used to getting his way, on and off of the ice. He helped put the Big, Bad Boston Bruins back on the map in 1970 and '72 with a pivotal role in two Stanley Cups, sandwiched around a remarkable season of 76 goals and 76 assists. In 1968–69, he became the first player to reach 100 points in a season, finishing with 126. His goal record that year stood until Wayne Gretzky's arrival a decade later.

Esposito couldn't be pushed off the puck in front, something the frustrated Soviet national team found out in 1972 when it thought it had crushed Team Canada's spirit. Esposito had a rich history with two other Original Six teams besides the Bruins, centring Bobby Hull in Chicago for a time up to his trade east in a 1967 blockbuster deal. After he and Bobby Orr restored Bruin pride, he joined the New York Rangers in another huge deal during 1975–76.

Esposito never took it easy on any goaltender, especially brother Tony of the Black Hawks, who shared a spot with Phil on two All-Star Teams. Phil

stayed on in a coaching and management capacity with New York and pulled off some big trades of his own, landing Marcel Dionne and sending a first-round draft choice to the Quebec Nordiques to secure coach Michel Bergeron.

Surviving an intense boardroom battle to determine who would be part of the expansion group that eventually was awarded the Tampa Bay Lightning in 1992, Esposito made some controversial moves such as signing Manon Rheaume as the NHL's first female goaltender. He then took his strong opinions to talk radio.

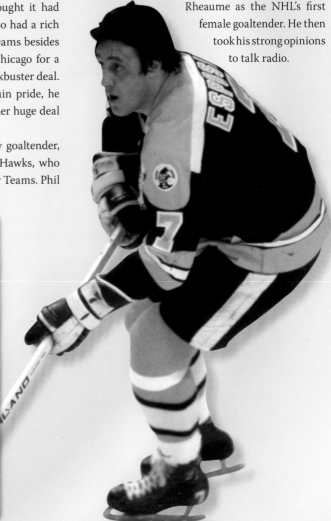

Bet you didn't know

Esposito's famous speech to rally Team Canada '72 after it was booed in Game 4 in Vancouver was not heard by his teammates. They had left the ice when a fired-up Esposito began chiding Canadian fans on live TV for their behaviour, and there was no dressing room monitor on which to see the sweaty, angry Espo's rant. When the country heeded his call, the Canadian team was already on its way to Moscow, but the thousands of telegrams of support it received from home showed them Esposito had swayed public opinion.

Bobby Clarke

Bobby Clarke was probably the best-protected skill player in NHL history. When he put together his 1,210-point NHL career, including back-to-back 100-point seasons in the mid-1970s, he did so with the Broad Street Bullies as his elite bodyguards. Philadelphia bulldozed to two Stanley Cups, while their captain made sure the club stayed together from the first day of training camp until the last sip of champagne from the Cup. Many of the champion Flyers still live together in the Philly area, a tribute to Clarke's insistence on a tight team bond.

Clarke learned a huge lesson in team dynamics in 1972, not long after joining the league. Working overtime to get a small role

on the Canadian team that would play the Soviets in the historic Summit Series, Clarke centred a line with Paul Henderson and Ron Ellis that became the team's most reliable two-way unit. Henderson became the scoring hero, but Clarke was credited with striking a nefarious and decisive blow against the Soviets by chopping down Valeri Kharlamov at the ankle.

Clarke earned the Hart Trophy three times, the first expansion-era player to win it. The Flyers' intimidation tactics were eventually overcome by Montreal in the late 1970s, but they would continue to be a big and heavy-handed team under Clarke's tenure as general manager.

Clarke left the organization briefly for executive positions with the Minnesota North Stars and Florida Panthers, but he always came back to Philly. Clarke had a couple of health scares early in his career, diagnosed as a diabetic in his teens and later, having a contact lens shatter in his eye during a game.

Bet you didn't know

Flyers general manager Bud Poile was skeptical of Clarke's ability to play through diabetes and passed on him with Philly's first pick in the 1969 draft. This despite Flin Flon Bombers coach Pat Ginnell taking Clarke from the small Manitoba town to the Mayo Clinic, where a doctor gave written assurance that Clarke could play with the condition. Poile needed to be convinced by a second specialist before taking Clarke with his next pick. Bob Currier, chosen by the Flyers ahead of Clarke, never played an NHL game.

Sidney Crosby

What has made Sidney Crosby so successful at a young age is not just his own talent. He seems to have absorbed, in equal amounts, the on-ice flair of his boss, Mario Lemieux, the off-ice charisma of Wayne Gretzky, and the fire of Phil Esposito. He took home the Mark Messier leadership award at the end of the 2009–10 season.

Where others of whom greatness was predicted either fell short or took a while to catch up to their own hype, Crosby was a scoring champion, most valuable player, Stanley Cup champion, and Canada's Olympic gold medal hero less than five years after making the NHL.

And he freely admits there is work to be done to improve his game, dedicating the

summer after the '09 Pittsburgh Penguins' Stanley Cup to doing better on faceoffs, resulting in a big jump in his winning percentage. Like Gretzky, Crosby learned some lessons from his first Cup defeat at the hands of the Red Wings in the '08 final, returning a year later to help beat the same team and become the youngest captain to hoist the big trophy. He was already the first teen scoring champion in any major pro sport when he had 120 points in 2006–07.

Though Pittsburgh management was congratulated for building a good, young team around the Nova Scotia-born Crosby, it won the right to pick through a lottery of non-playoff teams that followed the washed out 2004–05 season. Anaheim selected second and chose forward Bobby Ryan.

Bet you didn't know

The capacity for hockey crowds at the new home of the Penguins at Consol Energy Center has been set at 18,087. That's in tribute to Crosby's number 87 sweater, which will no doubt be responsible for many sellouts to come after the team moves there in October 2010. Crosby wears 87 because it's his birth date (8/7/87) and he signed one of his contracts for $8.7 million U.S. in 2007.

Peter Forsberg

Though Ornskoldsvik can be hard on North American tongues, Peter Forsberg made the place as familiar to North Americans as Moose Jaw or Rimouski. When he burst upon the NHL scene with the Quebec Nordiques as a point-a-game, Calder Trophy-winning centreman in the shortened 1994–95 season, he opened a door that soon had townsfolk Markus Naslund, the Sedin twins, and, most recently, Victor Hedman rushing in behind.

Forsberg had strong ties to Ornskoldsvik, a town of 28,000, and later in his career was often in a personal tug-of-war to play for the local Modo club team or the NHL. When he did venture across the ocean,

Forsberg was a force in the NHL and revered in Sweden for showing its players could excel with a physical game while still playing with a scoring touch.

Forsberg was commemorated on a Swedish stamp for a 1994 Olympic shootout goal against Canada that clinched gold. He came to the NHL the next year and joined the Colorado Avalanche after the team's transfer from Quebec. With a whopping 137 regular-season and playoff points, he was a huge part of the Avs' '96 Cup win and he would be part of another in 2001.

But as he suffered a series of injuries, he missed the entire following season and never played a full 82 games again. Among his many ailments were the removal of his spleen and a foot injury that hampered his trademark skating stride and saw him leave the NHL for good after 2007–08. His 2002–03 season produced his only Hart Trophy, with 106 points, as he beat out Naslund for the honour.

Bet you didn't know

The specifics of Forsberg's long history of foot problems can be traced to an abnormal arch that led to ankle tendons being stretched and damaged. He began experiencing difficulties with both feet and there was a long process of surgery and experimenting with several different skate boots to try to revive his career. Forsberg never really got the problem solved and refused to return to the NHL at less than 100 percent.

RIGHT WING

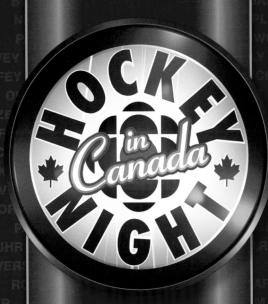

1. Gordie Howe
2. Maurice Richard
3. Bernie Geoffrion
4. Andy Bathgate
5. George Armstrong
6. Bill Cook
7. Charlie Conacher
8. Gord Drillon
9. Bill Mosienko
10. Bobby Bauer

1 Gordie Howe

The legendary Gordie Howe, otherwise known as "Mr. Hockey," played 26 seasons in the NHL, six more in the WHA, and a total of 34 seasons in professional hockey for a career that stretched over an unbelievable six decades. Think about it: Howe was 18 years old when he started his NHL career, and 52 when it ended. In the process, he became the only father to play with his sons, Mark and Marty.

"It was pretty special to play with the boys," said Howe in understatement.

Gordie could score goals, was a terrific playmaker, skated well, and was tough as nails, a gifted pugilist who was also famous for his flying elbows. In short, Howe could do it all. He was one of the greatest players of all time. No wonder they called him Mr. Hockey.

On top of all that, Howe, who shot right, would often switch around and shoot left. "In hockey, switcher hitters are as rare as snowflakes in July," the late Red Wings manager Jack Adams once said. "Gordie Howe was the best prospect I ever saw."

Howe won the Stanley Cup four times with the Detroit Red Wings and led them to a record seven straight first-place finishes between 1949 and 1955. He was a six-time winner of the Hart Trophy and six times led the NHL in scoring. He finished in the top five in league scoring for 20 straight seasons.

The native of Floral, Saskatchewan, who began skating when he was six by wearing adult-sized skates, started with the Red Wings in the 1946–47 season, his signing bonus that first season consisting of nothing more than a team jacket. One of the most prolific scorers in hockey history, Howe had only seven goals his rookie season and needed a couple of more years to really find his way.

Howe played right wing on the famed "Production Line," with centre Sid Abel and left wing Ted Lindsay, for a large part of his career. He became the NHL's all-time leading scorer until a kid named Wayne Gretzky, who just happened to idolize Howe, came along, entering the NHL just about the time Howe was leaving.

Howe's illustrious and lengthy career was almost cut short in the 1950 playoffs. Howe had finished third in league scoring that year, behind Lindsay and Abel. In the first game of the playoffs, Howe tried to check Toronto's Ted Kennedy, missed him, and crashed head-first into the boards, suffering a fractured skull that required surgery to relieve the pressure on his brain.

Howe didn't return that spring, but he recovered to continue his brilliant career. It was a chronic wrist problem that prompted Howe to first retire after 25 years in Detroit, following the 1970–71 season. He returned two years later with the Houston Aeros for a chance to play with his sons. Incredibly, he won two league championships in the WHA and was the most valuable player in 1974.

Howe played four seasons in Houston, then a couple in New England before the WHA merged with the NHL in 1979, after which Howe played his final season with the Hartford Whalers. Howe didn't just put in his time in that final season, either. At the age of 52, he played all 80 games, scoring 15 goals and earning 41 points.

His 1,767 NHL games are the most of any player, and his 26 NHL seasons is also a record. Howe stands third in NHL all-time scoring with 1,850 points, surpassed only by Gretzky and Mark Messier. Howe is second in goals to Gretzky with 801. Including regular season and playoff games, Howe played in

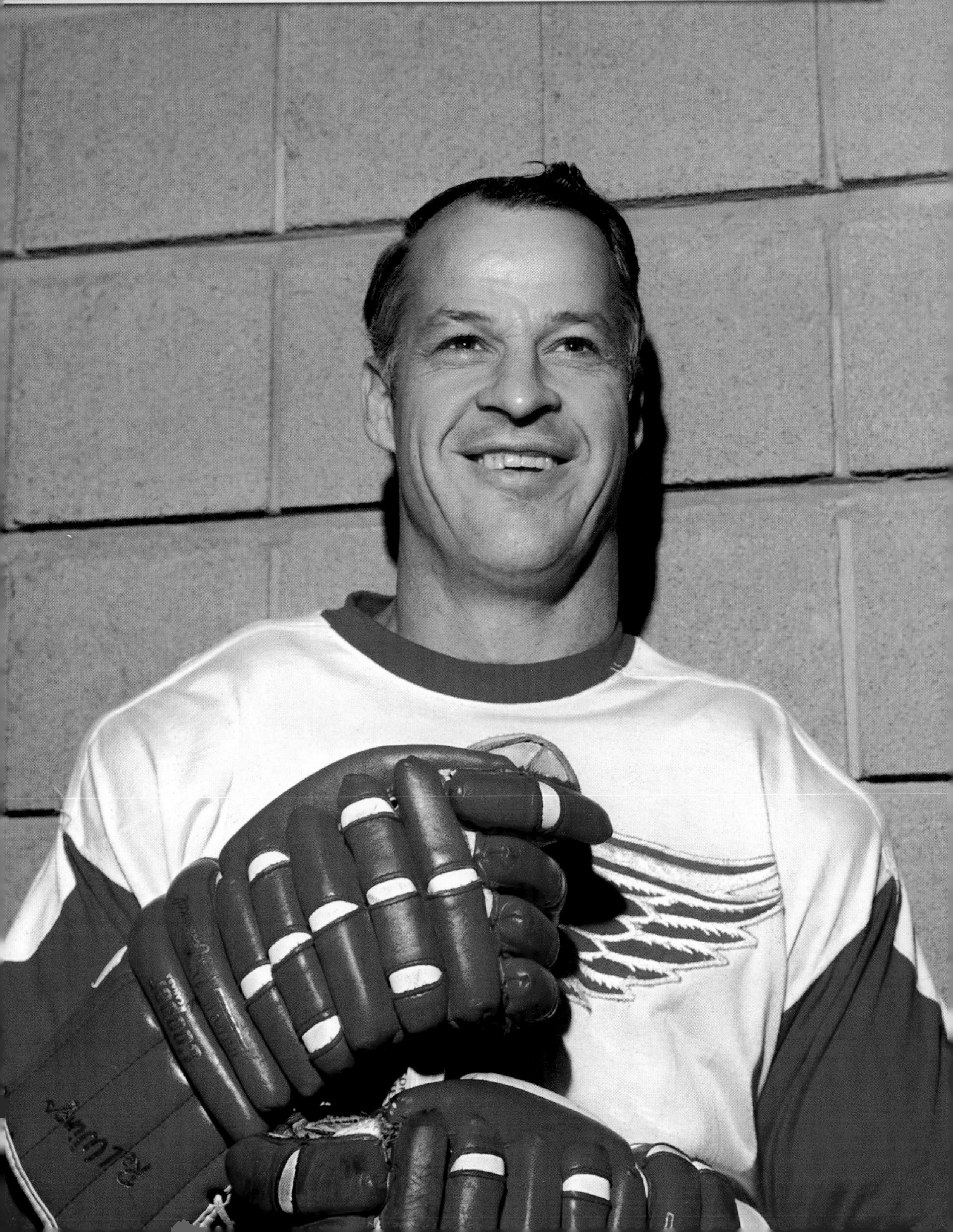

1,924 games, second only to Messier, scoring 869 goals, second to Gretzky, and 2,010 points, again third behind Gretzky and Messier.

Put his NHL and WHA numbers, regular season and playoffs, together and Howe had a staggering 1,071 goals and 2,589 points. He was an NHL First-Team All-Star a dozen times and was named to the Second Team nine times.

In 1997, Howe made a one-game, one-shift appearance with the Detroit Vipers of the IHL at the age of 69, becoming the only player to play in six decades. He was inducted into the Hockey Hall of Fame in 1972, between stops in the NHL and WHA. His number nine was retired by three teams—Detroit, Hartford, and Houston.

↻ Gordie Howe (left) hugs goalie Johnny Bower after the Leafs beat Detroit in a five-game Stanley Cup final in 1963. Frank Selke, Jr. is conducting the interview.

Bet you didn't know

The term "Gordie Howe Hat Trick" is used when a player scores a goal and an assist and has a fight—all in one game. Given the way Howe played, a prolific scorer and playmaker who wasn't afraid to scrap and once allegedly knocked out Rocket Richard, you would think Mr. Hockey had a ton of Gordie Howe Hat Tricks.

Alas, it appears that Howe had but two, both against the Maple Leafs. The first came on October 11, 1953, when he had a goal and an assist and fought Fern Flaman. The second was March 21, 1954, when he scored, had two assists, and fought Ted Kennedy after high-sticking him and clipping his ear. That was retribution for the 1950 incident in which Howe tried to check Kennedy but crashed heavily into the boards and suffered a fractured skull.

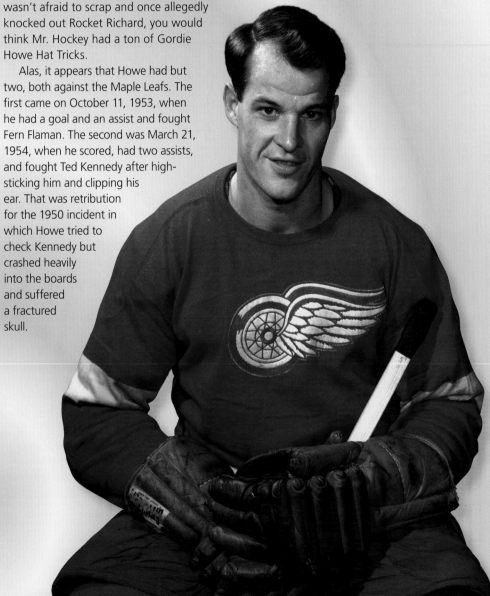

Maurice Richard

He was, of course, known as "The Rocket" and was nicknamed as such for his great speed. Richard was the complete package: he skated hard; he was physical; he was one of the greatest pure goal scorers ever in NHL history; he was a gifted playmaker. And he had piercing eyes that cut holes in an opponent.

"When he was coming down on you, the puck glued to the end of the stick, his eyes were flashing and gleaming like the lights on a pinball machine," said legendary goaltender Glenn Hall. "It was frightening."

Richard debuted with the Habs in 1942, but his first season was cut short because of a broken ankle. He scored 32 goals the following year, then became the first player in league history to score 50

goals. He did it in 50 games, playing on the "Punch Line" with Elmer Lach and Toe Blake.

During that 1943 season, Richard became the first player to register eight points in one game, a record that stood until 1976 when Darryl Sittler had a 10-point night for the Maple Leafs. Richard, who finished with 544 goals and 965 points, was a First Team All-Star eight times, and a Second Team All-Star six times. But he was also an all-star in some form for 14 straight seasons. He led the league in goal scoring five times and five times was runner up for the Art Ross Trophy as scoring champion. He was the first NHL player to score 500 goals.

Richard, who played his best in big games, won the Stanley Cup eight times with the Habs, including five in a row from 1956–60. He retired after that last win and was inducted into the Hockey Hall of Fame in 1961.

Bet you didn't know

When he first joined the Canadiens in 1942, Maurice Richard wore sweater number 15. After an ordinary season, in which he had some bad luck and injuries, he asked coach Dick Irvin if he could change his number to perhaps change his luck. He decided to switch to the number 9, which he made legendary in Canadiens history. And why 9? His daughter Huguette was born in 1943 and weighed nine pounds.

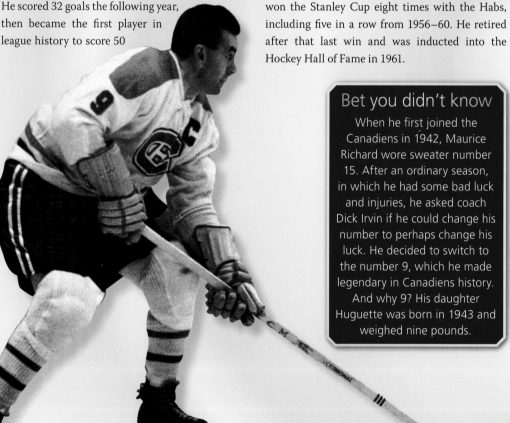

Bernie Geoffrion

The man who popularized the slap shot couldn't be known as anything other than "Boom Boom." Bernard Andre Joseph Geoffrion burst into the NHL in the 1950–51 season and ignited a trail of curiosity for this new, thunderous kind of shooting. The Montreal Canadiens' right-winger was the Calder Trophy winner after his first full season (1951–52) and by 1960 had his name on the Stanley Cup six times.

Geoffrion was one of the 12 players who played on Montreal's five straight Cup-winning teams between 1955 and 1960. Years later he would say: "As far as I am concerned, we had the best team ever in the NHL."

Oddly, he may be as well known for a feat that occurred when the Habs failed to defend in 1961—he completed that season as the NHL's second-ever 50-goal scorer. He fired 50 in 64 games, reaching the magic plateau that only long-time teammate Maurice Richard had ever seen, winning the Hart Trophy in the process. Geoffrion also had two Art Ross trophies to his credit, that 1960–61 season and an earlier honour in 1955.

He was elected to the Hockey Hall of Fame in 1972 but it was 34 more years before the Canadiens got around to retiring his number 5 sweater, sadly just hours after his death on March 11, 2006.

Bet you didn't know

At 33, Geoffrion announced his retirement in the spring of 1964 and went into coaching. He ran the Habs' AHL farm team, the Quebec Aces, for two seasons before returning as an active player with the New York Rangers in 1966. He scored 17 goals, then five, in those two seasons, and went back to coaching, first with the Rangers for a season and then for three more with the Atlanta Flames. He became the Canadiens' coach to start the 1979–80 season. "Boom Boom" stepped aside after 30 games because of a combination of team turmoil and health reasons.

Andy Bathgate

Not only does he remain one of the game's finest gentlemen, but Andy Bathgate was a model of consistency during an NHL career that spanned 19 years. Patrolling the right wing for the New York Rangers, the Winnipeg native, starting in 1955–56, finished in the NHL's top 10 of scoring nine straight times. The Rangers made the playoffs in only four of those years.

In an era of prolific scorers—the likes of Bobby Hull, Jean Beliveau, Boom Boom Geoffrion, Stan Mikita, and Gordie Howe were in their prime—Bathgate's results measure up. Despite finishing third in the scoring race to Dickie Moore and Beliveau in 1958–59, Bathgate was voted the winner of the Hart Trophy. By leading the NHL in assists with 56 in 1961–62, he shared the NHL scoring lead with Hull, but it was Hull who won the Art Ross because he had more goals: 50. Bathgate was runner-up to Howe the next season.

Bathgate also led the NHL in assists in 1963–64, a highlight season in which he was traded to the Toronto Maple Leafs and scored the Stanley Cup-winning goal against Detroit. It was the only Cup victory of his 1,069-game, 973-point career.

Bathgate was inducted into the Hockey Hall of Fame in 1978 and 31 years later, he and 704-game Rangers teammate Harry Howell had their sweaters (numbers 9 and 3, respectively) retired at Madison Square Garden.

Bet you didn't know

Nearly every hard-core hockey fan knows that goalie Jacques Plante started wearing a face mask on November 1, 1959, the first player of the modern era to do so. Why? The Habs' goalie was hit in the face and cut by a shot from the Rangers' star Andy Bathgate that night. After a delay of 20 minutes for stitches, Plante returned, wearing, much to the dismay of his coach, the famous facemask.

George Armstrong

⑤

The last Toronto captain to lift the Stanley Cup was thought by many to be an overachiever. Not a good enough skater, not a good enough player, so the story went.

George Armstrong, though, played far too long for that assessment to ever have a chance to stick. The longest-serving captain in Leafs history, 13 seasons from 1957–69, played all 1,187 NHL regular-season games of his career in Toronto, finishing with 713 points. More importantly, he was the leader of one of the Leafs' power eras, as Toronto took four Stanley Cups between 1962 and 1967. It wasn't the five-in-a-row Canadiens of the previous decade—who had beaten the Armstrong-captained Leafs for their last two wins in 1959 and 1960—but it was the franchise's last bona fide dominant period.

Armstrong never fired more than 23 goals in a single season, but it was his dependable style and character that carried the Leafs to those heights. Before he broke in with Toronto on a permanent basis in 1952, the Skead, Ontario, native had Memorial Cup (Toronto Marlboros), Allan Cup (Sr. Marlboros) and Calder Cup (Pittsburgh, AHL) victories on his resume.

Armstrong, who retired in 1971, was inducted into the Hockey Hall of Fame in 1975. He still holds the Toronto franchise records for most seasons played (21) and most games played (1,187).

Bet you didn't know

Armstrong's nickname, "Chief," is Hockey 101 knowledge, but the origin of the handle isn't quite as mainstream. According to the Leafs' website, Armstrong's became known as "Chief Shoot-the-puck" at a 1950 junior tournament, the name given to him by a native Canadian tribe from Alberta. The "Chief" part stuck partly because of his native heritage, but mostly for the leadership qualities the word conveys.

Bill Cook

Before there was an Art Ross Trophy for the NHL scoring title (the trophy was inaugurated in 1948), Bill Cook led the NHL in points on two occasions. The Hockey Hall of Famer from Brantford, Ontario, led the NHL in scoring in his rookie year, 1926–27 (also the inaugural year for his New York Rangers) and repeated the feat again in 1932–33 when he collected his second Stanley Cup with the Rangers. The icing on the cake was his overtime-winning goal to give the Blueshirts the Cup against Toronto.

Cook played on the Rangers' famed "Bread Line" with his brother Fred "Bun" Cook and Frank Boucher. It was in the NHL's heyday of famous lines, with the Leafs' "Kid Line" (Charlie Conacher, Busher Jackson, Joe Primeau) among them.

The Rangers won the Cup in Cook's second season, and his NHL career included 474 games, 229 goals, and 367 points. Cook was the oldest of three pro-playing brothers, a hard-shooting right-winger who interrupted his playing career for four seasons to serve for Canada in the Second World War.

After the war, he played for the Sault Ste. Marie Greyhounds and in Saskatoon of the WCHL, winning two scoring titles in Saskatchewan before being recruited by the Rangers at the age of 30.

Bet you didn't know

None of the Cook brothers— Bill, Bun, and Bud—had a given name that started with the letter B. Bill, of course, was William. Bud's first name was Alexander, and Bun (shortened from Bunny, as in "quick as a bunny," so named by a hockey writer) was born Frederick.

Charlie Conacher ⑦

We should all skate so poorly.

As a kid, future Hockey Hall of Famer Charlie Conacher was such a poor skater that he was put in goal so as not to drag down his team. But the "Big Bomber" was more determined than discouraged. One of 10 siblings, the lanky right winger was said to possess the hardest shot in hockey during his 12-season NHL career.

Goalies would endorse such status, as Conacher led the NHL in goal-scoring five times. His best campaign of the nine he played for the Toronto Maple Leafs was 36 goals in 47 games in 1934–35, one of the two seasons in which he also won the overall scoring title.

When he broke in at age 19 with the Leafs, in 1929–30, he was teamed with 18-year-old Busher Jackson and 22-year-old Joe Primeau to form the famous "Kid Line." Conacher earned one Stanley Cup with the Leafs, 1931–32, and finished his career playing a season for the Detroit Red Wings and two more for the New York Americans.

Part of a famous hockey family, Conacher and his brothers Lionel and Roy are all Hockey Hall of Fame members. Conacher's son Pete also played in the NHL, in the 1950s.

Bet you didn't know

Charlie Conacher's scoring prowess was eventually stopped by injuries, not goalies or checkers. During his career he endured the loss of a kidney from crashing the net, a broken collarbone, a shoulder separation, blood poisoning, and numerous fractures. He lost a final battle to throat cancer in 1967, leading to the establishment of the Charlie Conacher Research Fund that has raised millions of dollars in search of a cure. The NHL also gave out the Charlie Conacher Memorial Award between 1968 and 1984 for the player best exhibiting humanitarian and public service contributions.

Gord Drillon

Being compared to Charlie Conacher had its pluses and minuses for Gordie Drillon. The Moncton, New Brunswick, native joined the Leafs just as the dominant Conacher had departed. For a scoring right-winger to be mentioned in the same breath was an exceptional compliment. But the bar was set awfully high, and there were those who thought the six-foot winger—huge in those days—could have done more.

Still, Drillon produced impressive offence, scoring 20 or more goals five times in seven seasons, all in schedules that had fewer than 50 games. In back-to-back seasons during his career with the Leafs, he led the Stanley Cup playoffs in scoring, with seven post-season goals each time. Both years, however, the Leafs lost in the Cup final in 1938–39, and semi-finals the previous year,.

Leafs goalie Turk Broda said that Drillon was as pure a shooter as there was. "I don't think there's a player in hockey who can shoot the puck more accurately," Broda said. "Even if you leave him an opening the size of the puck, he'll hit it every time."

In his sixth season with the Leafs (1941–42), Drillon was benched by coach Hap Day during Toronto's historic comeback from 3–0 down in the Stanley Cup Final against

Detroit. But after the Cup was won, he was shipped to Montreal. There, he had one more productive year (50 points) before beginning three years of military service during the Second World War, effectively ending his career.

Bet you didn't know

It is now 72 years and counting since a Leafs player last won the NHL scoring title. The last? Gord Drillon, who scored 26 goals and 52 points in 48 games in his second season, 1937–38. It was also good enough for a First Team All-Star selection, and after incurring just two minor penalties all year, he earned the Lady Byng Trophy as well.

Bill Mosienko

Hall of Famer Bill Mosienko scored 258 goals during a rock-solid 711-game NHL career that spanned 15 seasons. A very small segment of it all—three goals in just 21 seconds—has made Mosienko part of the foundation of NHL history.

It was the most meaningless of games on March 23, 1952. Both Mosienko's Chicago Black Hawks and the New York Rangers were destined to miss the playoffs, yet both had one final regular-season game to complete. The Rangers' top two goalies were missing, Chuck Rayner with injuries and Emile Francis sent to the farm to help with a playoff run, so young goalie Lorne Anderson had his chance to prove he belonged.

After two periods that night, the Rangers had hammered Chicago goalie Harry Lumley for a 6–2 lead. But Black Hawks centre Gus Bodnar started winning faceoffs. For Mosienko's first two goals, at 6:09 and 6:20 of the third period, he took Bodnar passes and streaked in to beat Anderson. On the third, Bodnar won a faceoff and sent

the puck to left winger George Gee, who then sent it to Mosienko for the goal at 6:30.

The Winnipeg native had sparked a 7–6 Chicago win with his 29th, 30th, and career-high 31st goal of the season. Only 3,254 fans witnessed the feat.

Bet you didn't know

Despite playing on Chicago's high-profile "Pony Line" with Max and Doug Bentley, complete with all the attention from opponents, Mosienko had two seasons (1944–45 and 1947–48) in which he didn't incur a single minor penalty. He was the Lady Byng Trophy winner in 1945. He had Second Team All-Star selections in two years (1945, 1946) but awards were few and far between for the sad-sack Black Hawks of Mosienko's era. In his 15 seasons, he had only four opportunities to participate in the playoffs.

Bobby Bauer

As junior teammates with the Kitchener Greenshirts, Bobby Bauer, Milt Schmidt, and Woody Dumart were fast friends. As three budding Boston Bruins pros during the 1936–37 season, Providence coach Bert Leduc dubbed them the "Sauerkrauts," in consideration of each man's German heritage.

Shortened soon to just the "Kraut Line," the trio was long on results, sparked by Bauer, the small but clever right-winger. In 1938–39, the Krauts' second season, the Bruins won the Stanley Cup. They pulled it off again in 1941. The season in between, Schmidt, Dumart, and Bauer finished 1-2-3 in NHL scoring.

Bauer's fairly short career of 327 games—he retired at the peak of his performance to go into the skate business at home—consisted of 123 goals, 260 points, and a chemistry rarely matched in the NHL. Bauer was also a legendary player in terms of sportsmanship. He was the NHL's Lady Byng winner in 1940, 1941, and 1947, recording just 36 penalty minutes in his entire career.

He missed three seasons because of Royal Canadian Air Force service during the Second World War and rejoined the Bruins for two postwar seasons before returning home for good.

Bauer later coached senior hockey and twice in the Olympics for Canada. He remained involved in local teams and, after his unexpected death in 1964, was posthumously inducted into the Hockey Hall of Fame in 1996.

Bet you didn't know

As swan songs go, Bauer may have had the ultimate. Having been out of the NHL for nearly five years, he was re-united with Schmidt and Dumart for a regular-season game in which the "Kraut Line" was honoured by the Bruins. Schmidt scored early and Bauer scored late, giving Bauer a two-point night on March 18, 1952. That season, as a regular with the senior-league Kitchener Dutchmen, was Bauer's last as a player.

1. GUY LAFLEUR
2. MIKE BOSSY
3. JARI KURRI
4. BRETT HULL
5. TEEMU SELANNE
6. JAROMIR JAGR
7. YVAN COURNOYER
8. GLENN ANDERSON
9. PAVEL BURE
10. JAROME IGINLA

① Guy Lafleur

As a kid growing up in rural Thurso, Quebec, and like so many others playing hockey in the province, Guy Lafleur admired the legendary Jean Beliveau. "When I was a kid, everyone wanted to be Beliveau," he said.

Unlike the rest of those kids who wore Beliveau's number 4 and wished to one day live the dream of starring with the Montreal Canadiens, Lafleur actually made the dream come true. Drafted first overall by Montreal in 1971, Lafleur arrived with the Canadiens just as their legendary captain, Beliveau, was easing into retirement after another Stanley Cup win. And as with Beliveau before him—who also departed a Quebec City-team to join the Canadiens—Lafleur's arrival was highly anticipated by fans and management.

But then, that had always been the plan of Canadiens general manager Sam Pollock for years—a succession strategy for his glory teams that would see one great superstar ready to give way to the next. Pollock, of course, worked magic to acquire the first pick in that 1971 Entry Draft from the California Golden Seals—even going as far as sending a care package to the Los Angeles Kings to make sure they didn't slip beneath the Seals in the standings. He did it all to make sure he would get the Quebec Remparts star (although there was considerable speculation the Habs might draft Marcel Dionne).

Lafleur later said if the Canadiens hadn't acquired the pick, or hadn't selected him, he would have gone to the WHA's Quebec Nordiques before he would have played for the Seals or Kings. But that was a moot point. Somehow his arrival in Montreal never really seemed in doubt.

"The Flower" had an average start to his career in Montreal, at least by his standards, no doubt feeling the pressure of the great expectations thrust upon him. But in his fourth season he really began to blossom, as it were. That season, Lafleur scored 53 goals. He scored 56 the next year and 60 a few years after that as he put together a streak of six straight 50-plus goal seasons. He was the first player to have both 50 goals and at least 100 points in six straight seasons.

Lafleur was exhilarating to watch, one of the most exciting players in the game for years, with his blond locks flowing as he raced down the right wing, often unleashing a big slapshot from the faceoff circle, or cutting in to release a quick wrist shot. His other nickname was "le Demon Blond," or "The Blond Demon." Often overlooked with all of his goal-scoring exploits were Lafleur's exceptional playmaking abilities. As clichéd as it might sound, he really was a player who could lift fans out of their seats with his play.

He twice won the Hart Trophy during that six-year streak and three times was NHL scoring leader, and in each of those seasons he was a First Team All-Star. He was, of course, also a key ingredient in five Stanley Cup winning teams, winning the Conn Smythe Trophy once, with 26 points in 14 games.

He was the quickest player to reach 1,000 career points, doing it in 720 games, and his 1,246 points are the most in Canadiens' history. Lafleur was one of just eight players to win the Stanley Cup, Art Ross, and Hart Trophy all in the same season.

Don Cherry, who missed winning a Stanley Cup or two with his Boston Bruins because of Lafleur's brilliance, called him "the most exciting player outside Bobby Orr." Cherry recalled that Lafleur would always arrive at the rink early, around mid-afternoon on game days, and start to prepare mentally and physically. He would be dressed hours

before game time. "To see him going down the ice, that sweater rippling in the breeze, his hair flowing, it was a picture to behold," said Cherry.

According to the stories of the day, Lafleur lived large and enjoyed the Montreal nightlife for many years, but he changed his ways in 1981 after he was involved in a serious car accident. Lafleur spent 14 seasons with the Canadiens before retiring just 19 games into the 1984–85 season, just 33 years old.

He had just two goals and five points to start the season and felt his game had slipped. Lafleur's pride refused to allow him to be anything but the best.

"I don't believe any other player has come down in the past 12 years who could lift fans out of their seats like "Rocket" Richard," former NHL executive Brian O'Neill said the night the Canadiens honoured Lafleur. He remained out of the game for a little more than three years before making a

comeback at age 37 with the Rangers. He played a season in New York, scoring 18 goals and earning 45 points, and played two more seasons with the Quebec Nordiques before retiring for good. That choice brought a certain amount of closure for Lafleur, who ended his career where it had really begun—with a Memorial Cup win and a first selection in the 1971 draft.

As a kid, Lafleur lived and breathed hockey, spending every spare moment in the local arena. "When I was five, Dad gave me a heavy box for Christmas," Lafleur told the Hockey Hall of Fame. "When I opened it, there was only a piece of wood. I was so mad. Then he gave me another box and the skates were there. Dad used to build a rink behind our house every winter. That's where I started playing hockey. From the time I was seven, I used to sleep in all my equipment. That way, I was ready to play in the morning. We played hockey at noon and after school and we practiced until dark."

Interestingly, Lafleur was offered the opportunity to wear Beliveau's number 4 when he first arrived in 1971, a move endorsed by Beliveau himself. But Lafleur politely declined, in part out of immense respect for his idol and in part because the pressure of succeeding in Montreal was daunting enough. Fittingly, Lafleur made number 10 his number, which he had worn briefly in Junior B. It was retired by the Canadiens on February 16, 1985, the favourite number of another generation of Canadiens fans.

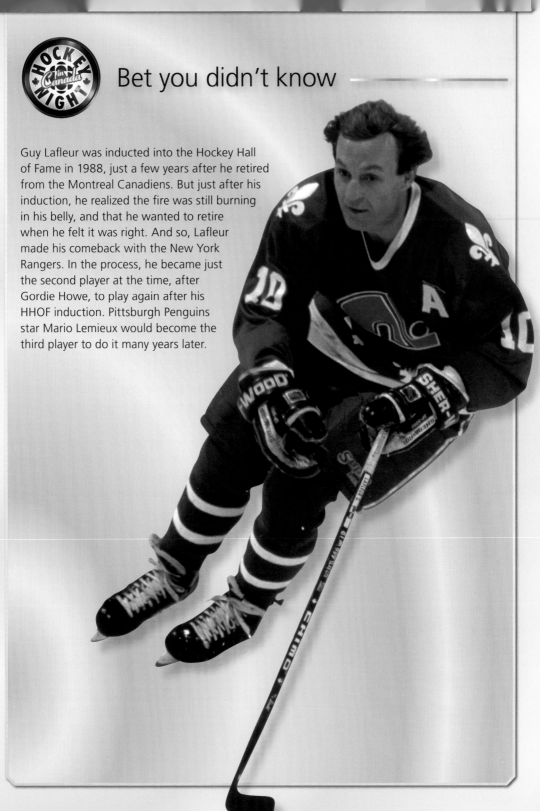

Bet you didn't know

Guy Lafleur was inducted into the Hockey Hall of Fame in 1988, just a few years after he retired from the Montreal Canadiens. But just after his induction, he realized the fire was still burning in his belly, and that he wanted to retire when he felt it was right. And so, Lafleur made his comeback with the New York Rangers. In the process, he became just the second player at the time, after Gordie Howe, to play again after his HHOF induction. Pittsburgh Penguins star Mario Lemieux would become the third player to do it many years later.

Mike Bossy

When it came to goal scoring, Mike Bossy was a natural. Blessed with a quick release shot—one teammate Kelly Hrudey once called the quickest he had ever seen—Bossy prided himself on seldom missing the net with his shots. Bossy has often said that he never tried to pick corners; he always wanted to get his shot on net and aimed at the middle. Funny, but he seldom missed the goaltender either.

Bossy, who was a big-time scorer as a 14-year-old junior in Laval, Quebec, had a terrific snap shot and a remarkable ability to pick corners and find openings. He was selected 15th overall by the New York Islanders in 1977, but some scouts questioned whether Bossy had the intestinal fortitude to be a good NHL player. Well, he immediately made an impact in the NHL, setting a then-rookie scoring record with 53 goals while playing on a line with Bryan Trottier and Clark Gillies, all three later making their way into the Hockey Hall of Fame.

Bossy won the Calder Trophy and went on to score 50 goals or more for nine consecutive seasons, which is quite the feat when considering he played only 10 seasons in total. That streak of nine consecutive is something not even Wayne Gretzky was able to accomplish, although he did score 50 goals or more nine times.

Bossy even scored 50 goals in 50 games in 1980–81, the first player to do it since Rocket Richard in 1944–45. Four times Bossy scored more than 60 goals in a season, including 69 in 1978–79.

Sadly, Bossy suffered from back woes and he retired at age 30. But he packed a lot into the decade that he played, winning the Stanley Cup four times with the Isles, winning the Conn Smythe Trophy once, and taking the Lady Byng three times.

Bossy played only 752 regular-season games, scoring 573 goals. He was also a big-game scorer, producing 85 playoff goals, which included 17 in three consecutive playoffs. He was inducted into the Hockey Hall of Fame in 1991 and his sweater number 22 was retired by the Islanders on March 3, 1992.

Bet you didn't know

Talk about your called shots. Not shy on confidence, Mike Bossy predicted prior to his rookie season with the New York Islanders that he would score 50 goals. He wound up scoring 53, a record for rookies that stood until 1992–93, when Winnipeg Jets freshman Teemu Selanne scored 76.

Jari Kurri

He may have been a witness to history, but Jari Kurri was also a major contributor. Kurri, of course, was the right winger for Wayne Gretzky for most of his glorious time in Edmonton, and again later with the Los Angeles Kings.

Kurri arrived in Edmonton in 1980, after being selected 69th overall by the Oilers that year. And his first season was a good one as he averaged a point a game. It was 19 games into the year, though, that he and Gretzky first played together on the same line. Kurri had a three-goal game that night, with Gretzky assisting on all three.

Kurri endured a 17-game scoring slump shortly after that but still managed to finish the season with 32 goals and 75 points. He went 10 straight seasons scoring 30 or more goals, including seven consecutive with 40-plus. He scored a career-high 71 goals in 1984–85, which at the time was a record for right wingers. He scored 68 goals the next season.

After Gretzky was traded to Los Angeles, Kurri wanted to follow but the Oilers wouldn't allow their rivals to acquire so much firepower. Kurri took a year off from the NHL to play in Italy and wound up with the Kings the following season. He played there for five seasons before being moved to the New York Rangers. He bounced to Anaheim and Colorado before retiring in 1998 with five Cup wins with the Oilers to his credit, the first Finn to ever win the Stanley Cup.

He was inducted into the Hockey Hall of Fame in 2001, again the first Finn so honoured.

Bet you didn't know

When he was a nine-year-old growing up in Helsinki, Finland, Jari Kurri played hockey for a team called the Toronto Maple Leafs. The local Jokerit hockey league used the names of NHL clubs for the kids' teams, and the team that selected Kurri wore Leafs uniforms.

Brett Hull

It's one thing to walk in your father's footsteps. It's another entirely to walk alongside him and to eventually earn your own superstar status. But that is exactly what Brett Hull, the son of Bobby, the legendary "Golden Jet," did. Heck, he even earned his own famous nickname, the "Golden Brett."

"I realized when I was 15 that it wasn't just going to be in hockey, but in life, if I didn't become Brett Hull and figure out who Brett Hull was—while still being honoured and loving the fact that I was Bobby Hull's son—I wasn't going to be anyone. And I kind of developed this game I played, just to be different."

While he had the famous bloodline, fame was not entirely expected for Brett, who was twice passed over in the draft. But after earning a scholarship to the University of Minnesota-Duluth, he was finally selected 117th overall by the Calgary Flames in 1984. There was never any doubt

about his skill; it was just whether he had the drive to make it as a pro.

Hull wound up scoring in his first regular-season game with the Flames and evolved into a scoring machine, just like his Dad, only different. Oh, he could score with a booming slapshot, but Brett would find open spaces and one-time shots past goaltenders. He used brains, not just brawn.

In 1988, looking for the missing pieces to a championship team, Flames general manager Cliff Fletcher dealt Hull to the St. Louis Blues where he blossomed, just as Fletcher predicted. Hull scored 41 goals his first season in St. Louis, then 72 while also winning the Lady Byng Trophy. The year after that he scored 86, earning the Hart and Pearson Trophies, and then adding 70 more in 1991–92.

After 11 seasons in St. Louis, Hull signed as a free agent with Dallas and won his first Stanley Cup in 1999, scoring a controversial overtime goal in the final game against the Buffalo Sabres. He signed with Detroit as a free agent in the summer of 2001 and won another Cup that season. Before retiring in the fall of 2005, he played five games with Phoenix, formerly Winnipeg, where his father had played part of his career. Brett wore his dad's number 9, which had been retired in between.

Brett Hull finished his career with 741 goals and once scored 50 in 49 games, becoming just the fifth player ever to reach 50 goals in 50 or fewer games, tying for fourth fastest ever. He also had 1,391 points and was inducted into the Hockey Hall of Fame in 2009.

Bet you didn't know

Bobby and Brett Hull became the first father-son combination to each record 1,000 career points, the son finishing with 1,391 points. When Brett scored his 600th goal, they became the only father and son combination to attain that lofty status as well.

Teemu Selanne

The "Finnish Flash," as he quickly became known, made a big splash when he debuted in the NHL in 1992–93. Selected 10th overall by the Winnipeg Jets in 1988, Teemu Selanne joined them four years later and proceed to turn the league on its collective ear, scoring a rookie-record 76 goals and 132 points to win the Calder Trophy in a season in which Eric Lindros also started his NHL career, albeit a few years younger. Selanne also made the First All-Star Team that rookie season.

Year two wasn't quite as good for Selanne, who severed his Achilles tendon in January and played in just 51 games, scoring 25 goals. After three and a half seasons in Winnipeg, he was traded to the Mighty Ducks of Anaheim, as they were then known. In his first two seasons with the Ducks, playing with Paul Kariya, Selanne had seasons of 51 and 52 goals and won the inaugural "Rocket" Richard Trophy as top goal scorer in 1999.

Selanne had stops in San Jose and a season in Colorado, where he joined Kariya, before returning to Anaheim, where he was a key player in their 2007 Stanley Cup championship. In the 2009–10 season, Selanne became the 18th player to pass the 600-goal plateau, finishing the year with 606 to pass countryman Jari Kurri (601) on that list. He also has 1,260 points.

Bet you didn't know

Teemu Selanne has been to five Olympic Winter Games representing Finland. At Vancouver, in 2010, he became the all-time points leader in the Games, finishing with 38 points in 31 games, two more than Hall of Famers Valeri Kharlamov of the Soviet Union and Harry Watson of Canada. Finland finished third in the tournament.

Jaromir Jagr

In his prime, Jaromir Jagr could dominate games. The fifth overall pick of the Pittsburgh Penguins in the 1990 draft was a gifted scorer and a brilliant playmaker. After scoring 27 goals in his rookie season, he went 15 straight years scoring 30 or more goals, peaking at 62 in 1996, the same season he finished with 87 assists and 149 points, both records for right wingers.

Jagr actually had a slow start to his first season, but the club quickly determined he was homesick for his native Czechoslovakia. They traded for centre and countryman Jiri Hrdina to help boost his spirits. It worked. A smooth skater, with size and the willingness to go into tough areas to score, Jagr quickly became a star, carrying the Penguins in the years that captain Mario Lemieux battled health and injury issues.

Jagr won four consecutive scoring titles and five overall, while he also won the Hart Trophy once and was a finalist five times. He won the Pearson Award three times. Five times in his career did Jagr surpass the 100-point plateau.

After 11 seasons and two Stanley Cup championships in Pittsburgh, Jagr was dealt to Washington because of contract reasons. He played there for two seasons before being moved to the New York Rangers in the third. He had three good seasons with the Rangers, then played two more seasons in the Russian league.

Jagr, who wore his number 68 as a reminder of the Soviet invasion of Prague in 1968, was part of the Czech Republic's gold-medal winning team in the 1998 Nagano Olympics. He finished his NHL career with 646 goals and 1,599 points, a dynamic star in his day.

Bet you didn't know

Early in his career, when Jaromir Jagr was playing with Mario Lemieux, someone with a little too much time on his hands figured that he could rearrange the letters in Jagr's first name to spell: Mario Jr.

Yvan Cournoyer

With a nickname like "The Roadrunner," it goes without saying that Yvan Cournoyer had good wheels. And that is about all scouts thought Yvan Cournoyer would ever have. Okay, they agreed he had good hands and could score and certainly skate, but at 5'7", 170 pounds, there was a concern he might not be big enough to survive the NHL wars.

Well, he proved them wrong. Oh, did he prove them wrong. Cournoyer wound up winning the Stanley Cup 10 times with the Montreal Canadiens and was one of the more prolific scorers in franchise history. He even wore the captain's C, taking over from Henri Richard in 1975.

Cournoyer had a great junior career with the Montreal Junior Canadiens. He joined the big club in 1963 for a handful of games and the following season full-time save for a few games with the AHL Quebec Aces. He had very good seasons of 25 and 28 goals, but he really took off in the 1968–69 season when Claude Ruel took over as coach. That year, Cournoyer had 43 goals and 87 points. In the 1971–72 season he had 47 goals, which helped to earn him an invitation to Team Canada for the Summit Series with the Soviet Union.

Cournoyer won the Conn Smythe Trophy in 1973, when he had 15 goals and 25 points during the Canadiens' Stanley Cup run. Back misery and a couple of operations eventually forced him to retire at the age of 35, after 15 seasons. But by then his name was among the all-time Canadiens greats on the goal-scoring list, and he was inducted into the Hockey Hall of Fame in 1982. He may not have been big enough, but he was certainly good enough.

Bet you didn't know

According to the Hockey Hall of Fame archives, when Yvan Cournoyer was playing for the Montreal Junior Canadiens, his legs were so thick he had to have his hockey pants altered. He also reportedly used to shoot a four-pound lead puck that helped to improve the velocity of his shot.

Glenn Anderson

When it came to playing in big games, Glenn Anderson was always at his best. Indeed, Anderson had a knack for scoring big goals. He had five career playoff overtime goals, which ranked third all-time to "Rocket" Richard, who had six, and Joe Sakic, who had eight. He also had 17 playoff game-winning goals, fifth best of all-time.

Anderson was blessed with great speed and was a swift, smooth skater. A left-hand shot, he played the right wing and would use his speed and skill to power down the right wing and cut in to the goal.

Edmonton's fourth-round pick in 1979, Anderson joined Canada's national team and played in the 1980 Lake Placid Olympics. He joined the Oilers in 1980–81

and remained there for 11 seasons, winning the Stanley Cup five times. Part of that great Oilers' nucleus, he also won the Canada Cup twice, in 1984 and '87.

Twice during those years with the Oilers he scored 54 goals and three times he had more than 100 points. Anderson was dealt to the Toronto Maple Leafs in 1991 and helped the Leafs through a couple of successful seasons in which they advanced to the Stanley Cup semi-finals. In 1994 he was traded to the New York Rangers, where he hooked up with several former Oilers, including Mark Messier, and helped lead the Rangers to their first Stanley Cup win in 54 years.

Anderson had a couple of stops with St. Louis and a brief return to Edmonton before retiring in 1996 with 498 goals and 1,099 points. A free spirit, Anderson was most focused when it came to playing in big games. He was inducted into the Hockey Hall of Fame in 2008.

Bet you didn't know

Glenn Anderson grew up in Burnaby, British Columbia, but he wasn't the only famous son to emerge from the city. A childhood friend was actor Michael J. Fox. Anderson claimed that he himself wasn't particularly enthused with hockey at an early age because he didn't like early mornings and he wasn't an especially good skater. "The first goal I ever scored," he said, "was in my own net."

Pavel Bure

Pavel Bure had tremendous speed and always seemed to find another gear to get away from defenders. Bure, who was nicknamed "The Russian Rocket," was the type of player who could bring fans to their feet. He would often drift around the ice without interest or purpose, then suddenly turn on the jets, grab a loose puck, and speed up the ice to score on a fast break.

Bure starred in the 1989 World Junior Championships for the Soviet Union, playing on a line with Alexander Mogilny and Sergei Fedorov. He was drafted by the Vancouver Canucks 113th overall in 1989 and joined them in the 1991–92 season, scoring 34 goals and 60 points and winning the Calder Trophy. The following seasons he took it up another

notch and put together back-to-back 60-goal, 100-plus point seasons, leading the Canucks to the Stanley Cup Final in 1994, where they lost in seven games to the New York Rangers.

That spring, Bure led the Canucks to an upset win over Calgary, scoring the series-winning goal in double overtime in the seventh game. He had 16 goals and 31 points in 24 post-season games. Bure was slowed for a couple of seasons because of knee issues, but he bounced back in the 1997 season, his last in Vancouver, with 51 goals. But Bure soured on Canucks management, sat out part of the next season, and demanded a trade, which he eventually got, to the Florida Panthers. But he re-injured his knee and appeared in only 11 games, scoring 13 goals. He bounced back again the following season, though, leading the league with 58 goals. He scored 59 the year after that.

Bure was traded to the Rangers at the deadline in 2002 and missed most of the following season with another knee injury before retiring. He played for Russia in the 1998 Winter Olympics, winning a silver medal after losing to Dominik Hasek and the Czech Republic, 1–0, in the gold-medal game.

Bet you didn't know

Pavel Bure came from an athletic family. His father, Vladimir, was a swimmer who took part in three Olympic Games. He won a bronze medal in 1968 in Mexico and three more medals in 1972 in Munich. Pavel's brother, Valeri, enjoyed a successful NHL career himself with the Montreal Canadiens, Calgary Flames, Florida Panthers, and St. Louis Blues.

Jarome Iginla

Jarome Iginla had an assist in his first NHL game and a goal in his second. One day he was literally playing junior hockey and watching the Calgary Flames on the highlights, and the next night he was playing for them against the Chicago Blackhawks in the playoffs.

Iginla, who was drafted by the Dallas Stars 11th overall in 1995 after twice winning the Memorial Cup with Kelowna, was obtained by the Flames in a trade for centre Joe Nieuwendyk. After that two-game playoff debut, Iginla played full time the next season for the Flames, scoring 21 goals and 50 points. He reached star level in 2002 when he led the league in scoring with 52 goals and 96 points.

That spring he won the Art Ross Trophy, Richard Trophy, and Pearson Award after earlier capturing gold with Canada at the Salt Lake City Olympics.

Two years later, Iginla tied for the league lead with 41 goals, but more importantly led the Flames to the Stanley Cup Final (their first playoff appearance since his debut in 1996). Iginla had 13 goals and 22 points in 26 post-season games, but the Flames fell one win short, losing to Tampa in seven games.

Iginla was again a finalist for the Hart Trophy in 2008, as he had been in 2002, reaching the 50-goal plateau one more time and finishing with a career-high 98 points.

Bet you didn't know

Iginla's full name is Jarome Arthur-Leigh Adekunle Tij Junior Elvis Iginla. Each name has a special meaning. Arthur-Leigh was his father's middle name. Adekunle was his father's first name in Nigeria before he came to Canada and changed his name to Elvis. Tij was the name of his father's father in Nigeria and Jarome named his son that, as well. Iginla means "big tree."

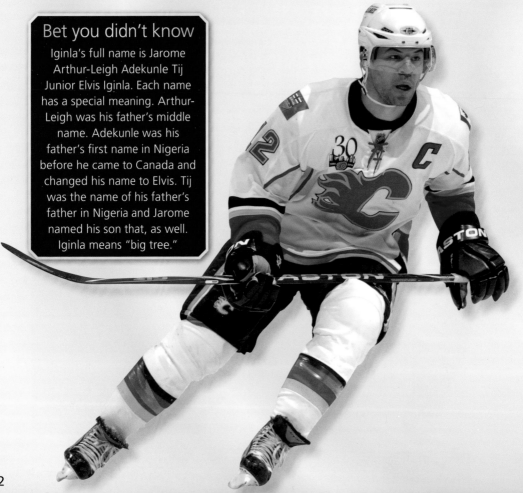

ORIGINAL SIX

LEFT WING

1. **BOBBY HULL**
2. **FRANK MAHOVLICH**
3. **HARVEY "BUSHER" JACKSON**
4. **TED LINDSAY**
5. **DICKIE MOORE**
6. **HECTOR "TOE" BLAKE**
7. **JOHNNY BUCYK**
8. **DOUG BENTLEY**
9. **DICK DUFF**
10. **AURELE JOLIAT**

1 Bobby Hull

When you think of Bobby Hull you automatically think of his slap shot. That would be the actual shot, which was a howitzer, and not the cult hockey movie.

Hull wasn't the first to use the slap shot, but he might have been its most effective practitioner, certainly in his day. For 16 seasons in the NHL and another seven in the WHA, Hull put the fear of God into goaltenders with that shot, many of whom played the game without a mask. And he scored goals in abundance.

Nicknamed the "Golden Jet" because of his blond hair and powerful stride, Hull was a strong skater who was also quick (they used to joke he had huge forearms like the cartoon character Popeye) and who carried a big, curved stick. He led the NHL in goal-scoring seven times, was the third player in NHL history to score 50 goals in a season, and the first to score more than 50, recording a record 54 in the 1965–66 season.

Hull was also the first NHL player to score 50-plus goals in a season more than once, doing it five times, including 58 goals during the 1968–69 season. Legendary hockey writer Rex MacLeod once described Hull's big shot as being "invisible" and later in his career, as Hull was slowing down, MacLeod said it was "merely a blur."

Hull, who scored 610 goals in the NHL, was a player who could lift fans out of their seats, rushing down the left wing, powering by defenders, crossing the blue line, and unleashing a booming slap shot—a hold-your-breath moment for the goalies and the fans. Not surprisingly, he was accused of placing the odd high shot around the ears of the goaltender early in a game to get him somewhat unnerved.

"I just tried to intimidate a goalie to the point where I had the edge," he said. "I would often purposely whistle the puck past the goaltender's ear...if I didn't like a particular defenceman I'd purposely shoot right at him. I'd keep it fairly low and that player was much easier to handle the rest of the night. Man cannot score 50 goals just on talent alone."

Hull won the NHL scoring title three times, the Lady Byng Trophy once, and the Hart Trophy twice. Ten times he was named to the First All-Star Team, twice to the Second Team. He was runner-up to Frank Mahovlich for the Calder Trophy in his rookie season, 1957–58, when he scored 13 goals and had 47 points.

Hull improved on his goal totals the following season, bumping up to 18 and 50 points. But it was his third season in which he really hit his stride. Hull had 39 goals and 81 points and won his first Art Ross Trophy playing on a line with Bill Hay and Murray Balfour, otherwise known as "The Million Dollar Line."

"What sticks out in my memory, even after Stanley Cups, 50-goal years, and playing for my country, is my third year in the NHL, when I first learned all about the game, how it should be played, and that I could entertain people," Hull said. "We would get 18,000 or more in Chicago and they weren't coming to see Montreal or Boston or Toronto. They were coming to see us. They couldn't wait for the next game because we entertained. It was a great feeling."

Hull's numbers dipped slightly the following season, but it was capped off by his lone Stanley Cup win in 1961 and the Hawks' first win since 1938. The following season he reached 50 goals for

⊃ Bobby Hull (left) is checked by Toronto's Jim Dorey.

the first time. Remember, too, that Hull had earned special attention on the ice, with opposition teams assigning annoying shadows to try to shut him down. In Toronto, he always played against Ron Stewart; in Detroit it was Bryan "Bugsy" Watson; and in Montreal it was Claude Provost.

After a trip to the Cup Final in 1965, and a disappointing semi-final loss to the Maple Leafs in 1967, when the Hawks were favoured to win the Cup, Hull scored a then-record 58 goals in the 1968–69 season. He was strong enough that his shot was always dangerous, but it had become even more so when teammate Stan Mikita happened upon the curve stick in practice quite by accident several years earlier. Mikita had tried to break his stick, but instead the blade curved. He finished practice using the bent blade and was intrigued by the results, with the puck able to rise or dip and utterly confound the goaltenders.

All of a sudden, the "banana curve" was in vogue. After that, players would soak their sticks in water, then jam them under a door and warp the blade. Hull helped lead the Hawks to the Final again in 1971, scoring 11 goals in 18 games, but they were upset by Montreal in seven games thanks to a dominating performance from rookie goaltender Ken Dryden.

It was in 1972 that Hull made history of a different kind. On June 27 of that year, he was given $1 million by the upstart World Hockey Association to lure him away from Chicago and put the league on the map. Then the Winnipeg Jets signed him to an additional $1.8 million deal. Chicago, like a lot of NHL teams, didn't think the WHA would fly and did little to persuade Hull to stay in the Windy City.

"I think they thought I was playing a game and that the WHA never would come about," Hull said years later. "They didn't think I would leave Chicago. The previous autumn I had a meeting with them and said I would like to finish my career in Chicago. That was 1971 and I wanted five more years. The WHA knew my contract was up and they came after me. I told the Hawks to offer me a contract but they never did until the day before I left for Winnipeg, and by then I had gone too far to turn Winnipeg down."

Hull said he would have stayed in Chicago for $250,000.

A few months after jumping to the WHA, Hull was in the middle of another storm, this one on the national stage, when he wasn't allowed to play in the historic Canada–Soviet Union Summit Series. Only NHL players were permitted to play, which prompted protests all the way to the federal government. Hull did get his chance two years later when a team of WHA players took on the Soviets and in 1976 in the Canada Cup tournament, in which he was one of the top stars for Canada and had five goals in seven games.

In the WHA, Hull scored 303 goals in 411 games, was twice named league MVP, and twice won the Avco Cup league championship. Four times he scored 50 or more goals, including 77 in 1974–75 while playing alongside Anders Hedberg and Ulf Nilsson with the Jets. After the WHA merged with the NHL in 1979, Hull played 18 games for Winnipeg but was traded to Hartford to play with Gordie Howe. He played just nine games with the Whalers before retiring.

When he left Chicago, Hull's 604 goals ranked second all-time behind Howe, but he was passed over the years by a number of players, including his son, Brett, who ranks third all-time behind Wayne Gretzky and Howe with 741 goals. Bobby Hull was inducted into the Hockey Hall of Fame in 1983.

Hull on a solo dash down the left wing.

Hull comes around the Toronto net while being checked by Rick Ley.

Bet you didn't know

Even though Bobby Hull was known as "The Golden Jet" because of his blond locks, Hull battled a receding hairline for much of his career and even took to wearing a hair piece while he was playing in the WHA. One night, in a game against the notoriously tough Birmingham Bulls, Hull became involved in a skirmish with Dave Hanson, who starred in the movie *Slap Shot*, and had his toupee pulled off.

"I forgot to glue the thing on, and when I got in this little skirmish a guy grabbed it and threw it on the ice," Hull told the late Rex MacLeod. Former Bulls coach John Brophy once said Hanson pulled on Hull's hair, had the toupee come off in his hand, looked at in horror, as though he had pulled out Hull's actual hair, and threw it to the ice.

"I kept circling it, moving guys out of the way and telling them to be sure not to step on it," Hull told MacLeod.

Said Hanson, "In the middle of the melee we both stopped. All the screaming stopped and I look up and Bobby doesn't look the same as when we started. I look at my hand and I had just pulled off his toupee…I was a bit shocked. I threw it on the ice."

2 Frank Mahovlich

Class and endurance—those are the qualities that allowed Frank Mahovlich to survive a hockey player's nightmare of scorn from fans and alienation from a coach.

Survive them the "Big M" did, becoming an easy selection to the Hockey Hall of Fame in 1981, three years after his career was over with 533 goals and 1,103 points in 1181 regular-season NHL games.

The big left-winger broke in full time with the Toronto Maple Leafs at the age of 19 in 1957–58. He scored regularly enough early in his career, but the 1960–61 season illustrated the struggle within. Mahovlich had finally found an elite stride in the NHL. He had 48 goals with two games remaining, and Maurice Richard's league record of 50 seemed easily within reach.

Mahovlich didn't score again that season.

From there, the fans seemed fickle and never quite satisfied. Taskmaster coach "Punch" Imlach criticized and picked on him, leading to serious bouts of depression in 1964 and again in 1967. Mahovlich said later he and Imlach didn't speak for five full years.

After four Stanley Cups, the Leafs traded Mahovlich in a huge deal with Detroit, and the graceful skater and scorer finally found some happiness. He gave the Wings major production, like 1968–69's 49-goal season.

The nine-time NHL all-star was traded a second time to Montreal in January 1971 and won two more Cups with the Habs, including his first season when he led the league in playoff scoring with 14 goals and 27 points in 20 games.

After the 1973–74 season, Mahovlich made the jump to the WHA and played four seasons with the Toronto Toros/Birmingham Bulls organization before retiring. He scored 171 points in his two Toros seasons.

Senator Frank Mahovlich was appointed to Parliament's upper chamber in 1998.

Bet you didn't know

The "Big M"'s rookie season of 20 goals and 36 points (1957–58) was good enough to win the Calder Trophy. Among those he beat out for the NHL's best-rookie award was Bobby Hull.

③

Harvey "Busher" Jackson

Style was synonymous with the career of Harvey "Busher" Jackson.

The Toronto native broke in with the Leafs as an 18-year-old in the 1929–30 season and became the NHL's youngest-ever scoring champion at the time of his league-leading 53 points in 48 games of 1931–32. That was also the year of his one and only Stanley Cup win.

Jackson had flare on the ice as a great rusher with a superb backhand, and off it as well with expensive taste in cars and an attraction to social events nationwide.

As part of the Leafs' famous "Kid Line" with Joe Primeau and Charlie Conacher, the left-winger was one of the great stars of his era. And when Primeau retired in 1936, Jackson played a year with his brother Art and then moved to another high-scoring unit with Syl Apps and Gord Drillon.

Leafs boss Conn Smythe, however, didn't care for Jackson's style, especially off the ice, and dealt him to the New York Americans for superstar "Sweeney" Schriner after 10 seasons. He played two more years in the Big Apple, then three more with the Boston Bruins before retiring with totals of 241 goals and 475 points in 633 NHL games.

Bet you didn't know

Jackson died of a liver ailment in 1966 without realizing his dream of making it to the Hall of Fame. When he was selected (along with Terry Sawchuk) to the class of 1971, five years after his death, Smythe resigned as chairman of the Hall's governing committee. Smythe's bitterness over Jackson's off-ice lifestyle had simmered for almost 40 years. "Standards are going down everywhere today," Smythe said in a Canadian Press story of June 12, 1971.

Ted Lindsay

Never judge a competitor by his size—this would have been by far the best way to approach Ted Lindsay on the ice. Once known as "Terrible-Tempered Ted," "Terrible Teddie," and even "Scarface" (he is said to have stopped counting after 400 facial stitches), the shortest version, "Terrible Ted," was the one that stuck.

A 5'8" left-winger who could beat you on the score sheet and in the corners, Lindsay did well enough in his first two NHL seasons. In his third, however, he was moved to a line with Sid Abel and Gordie Howe, and the threesome became the famous "Production Line," partly because of scoring and partly because the players belonged to Detroit, the nation's automotive capital.

Lindsay's 33 goals led the NHL in 1947–48, and in 1949–50 he won the Art Ross Trophy with 78 points in 69 games. His linemates were second and third en route to Detroit's Stanley Cup championship.

Eight times a First Team All-Star, Lindsay helped the Wings claim four Cups. He had his best-ever points season, 85, in 1956–57, but his reward, largely due to his key role in organizing the earlier version

of the NHL Players Association, was a banishment trade to sad-sack Chicago, where his clout among league players would be diminished.

Lindsay gutted it out for three seasons in the Windy City, then retired. Abel, then Detroit's coach, convinced him to come back for one final year with the Wings after four seasons off ice. "Terrible Ted" helped Detroit finish first that year, contributing 28 points.

With a final tally of 379 goals and 851 points and 1,068 games, including 1,808 penalty minutes, Lindsay was inducted into the Hall of Fame in 1966. In 2010, his all-faceted game and union stewardship was acknowledged by the NHLPA, which renamed its annual most-outstanding-player award the Ted Lindsay Award.

Bet you didn't know

"Terrible Ted"'s reputation certainly lives on, but despite being as emotional and smashed-mouth as he could be on the ice, he led the NHL in penalty minutes only once during his 17-season career (184 PIMs in Chicago, 1958–59). He did, however, exceed 100 PIMs 10 times, including his second-highest-ever total of 173 in his last season, at the age of 39.

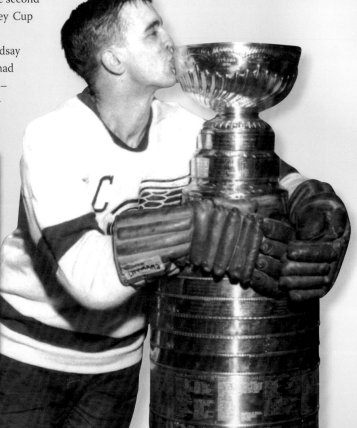

Dickie Moore

Could there be a better job in hockey than skating on a line with a "Rocket" and a "Pocket Rocket"?

Dickie Moore had that job and the rest of the NHL was in awe of the Montreal Canadiens' five-straight Stanley Cups, 1956–60.

The slick left-winger, who also had speed and grit, made the jump from junior (and a Memorial Cup victory) in 1951–52, joining the Habs at Christmas. With Elmer Lach and Maurice Richard as linemates part of that season, he scored 18 goals and 33 points.

Injuries limited Moore's playing time for the ensuing two seasons, but he eventually wound up skating with Henri and Maurice Richard for nine seasons. During the

third year of the five-straight Cup wins, Moore led the NHL in goals, with 36, and won his first of two consecutive Art Ross Trophies.

After the 1962–63 season, during which Moore scored 24 goals, the Habs were set to trade him, but he refused to be moved and retired instead. The Toronto Maple Leafs grabbed the retired left-winger in the intra-league draft of 1964, and "Punch" Imlach convinced a hurting Moore to give it another shot. Despite a bad kneecap, among other ailments, Moore managed 38 games and returned for Toronto's playoffs. Still hobbled, he retired again before a swan-song year in St. Louis after expansion in 1967.

Moore, who was inducted into the Hall of Fame in 1974, finished with 261 goals and 608 points in 719 NHL regular-season games, plus 110 points in 135 playoff games.

Bet you didn't know

After two years of his second retirement from the NHL, Moore returned again, this time to the St. Louis Blues during the league's first expansion year. Who instigated Moore's comeback? It was Cliff Fletcher, who was working for Scotty Bowman and the Blues. Moore worked out, lost 20 pounds, and joined the Blues in December, scoring eight points the rest of the season. But he was extraordinarily effective in the playoffs, recording 14 points as St. Louis made it all the way to the Cup Final.

Hector "Toe" Blake

Even without the famous fedora or his iconic status behind the bench of the Montreal Canadiens, Hector "Toe" Blake was a bona fide Hall of Famer for his playing career alone.

His coaching record, which brought the Canadiens eight Stanley Cups in 13 seasons, overshadowed his heady days as a Montreal left-winger. Blake's 12 full-time seasons in the NHL produced 235 goals and 527 points in 577 games and an impressive 62 points in 58 more playoff contests.

Blake's first full season was 1936–37 and in his third season he won the Hart Trophy and the scoring title with 47 points in 48 games. He had turned into such an impact player that "The Old Lamplighter" became his nickname. In 1943, Canadiens coach Dick Irvin moved Blake to a line that paid big dividends. With Elmer Lach and Maurice Richard, the "Punch Line" led the Habs to Stanley Cups in 1944 and 1946. Blake had the Cup-winning goal in both playoff runs.

In the season in between, the trio was 1-2-3 in NHL scoring as Blake helped Richard become the NHL's first 50-goal scorer.

Under Irvin, Blake was the Canadiens' captain until his retirement in 1948. That season, in January, Blake was checked by Bill Juzda, broke his leg, and played no more in the NHL, turning to coaching instead. He honed his craft in the minors until he took the reins of the Canadiens in 1955 and the rest, as they say, is history.

Inducted into the Hall as a player in 1966, Blake received the Order of Canada before his death in 1995.

Bet you didn't know

Toe Blake is about as synonymous as it gets with the Montreal Canadiens, yet it was another team that orchestrated his NHL debut. While playing with the senior Hamilton Tigers, Blake signed as a free agent with the rival Montreal Maroons. He played eight games but had little bearing on the Maroons' Stanley Cup win in 1935. In order to land top goalie Lorne Chabot, the Maroons traded Blake to the Canadiens late in the 1935–36 season.

Johnny Bucyk

"Better with age" goes a long way to describe Hall of Fame left-winger Johnny Bucyk. The Edmonton native arrived in the NHL at the age of 20. The year was 1955. After two seasons establishing himself with the Detroit Red Wings, Bucyk was offered up as compensation so the Wings could obtain the player they really wanted—goalie Terry Sawchuk.

And so Bucyk went to Boston in a June 1957 trade and never left. Through a run of eight out-of-playoff seasons, Bucyk laboured away with an honest and very good career, reaching 20 goals six times. But when the Bruins caught fire in the post-expansion era, it brought a pair of Stanley Cups and a lot of recognition.

Bucyk elevated his game to match the better players around him, and reached a pinnacle of 51 goals in the 1970–71 campaign. That season, seven of the top 10 NHL scorers were from Boston, including the top three—Phil Esposito, Bobby Orr, and Bucyk.

Bucyk was 35 years old at the time of his first Cup win, and his successes included the Lady Byng Trophy that season and also in 1974. By the time he retired in 1978, he had spent 23 NHL seasons accumulating several Bruins records: 1,540 games played, 556 goals, 1,369 points, plus 103 more points in 124 playoff games.

Bucyk was inducted into the Hockey Hall of Fame in 1981.

Bet you didn't know

Bucyk's number 9 was retired by the Bruins in 1978. And on his 1958–59 hockey card, for his second season in Boston, it was revealed (despite his two later Lady Byng Trophies) that his "pals call him 'The Beast,' because he hits so hard." Bucyk's penalty-minute totals declined markedly as his career progressed.

Doug Bentley

Proving that scouting errors and oversights aren't exclusive to the modern era, Doug Bentley's mercurial NHL career with the Chicago Black Hawks was largely at the expense of the Boston Bruins, who originally dropped him from their negotiation list.

The pride of Deslisle, Saskatchewan, from a family of 13 children, realized an NHL first in 1942: Three Bentley brothers, Doug, younger Max (an eventual Hall of Famer like Doug) and older Reggie, all played on the same line for the Hawks.

The line lasted only 11 games, the length of Reggie's stay in the NHL, but that 1942–43 season was historic as Doug won the NHL scoring title with 33 goals and 73 points, becoming the first Chicago player to do so.

Bentley, a small but complete player, followed that performance with a league-leading 38 goals in 1943–44, though he lost the scoring title by five points to Boston's record-setting Herb Cain. The Hawks also lost that Stanley Cup Final to the Montreal Canadiens. In the ensuing years, Bentley was an offensive force around the NHL. He led the league in assists for three straight seasons, 1946–49, and in a four-year span, finished sixth, third, second, and seventh in the overall scoring race.

By his retirement in 1954, Bentley had played 566 games, delivered 219 goals, and racked up 543 points. In all that time, he participated in just 23 playoff games, a comment on the lacklustre team performance in Chicago.

Bentley was inducted into the Hall of Fame in 1964.

Bet you didn't know

Doug Bentley's NHL career was interrupted for a full season, 1944–45, at the end of the Second World War. During the pre-season, the Black Hawks had travelled to Canada for an exhibition game, and when crossing the U.S.–Canada border on the way home, Doug was denied permission to leave Canada. That season, he played senior hockey for the Laura Beavers and tended to the family farm.

Dick Duff

Dick Duff broke into the NHL at the age of 19 with the Toronto Maple Leafs in 1955 and was among the wave of junior grads credited with rebuilding the pride of the franchise in the late 1950s. He earned full-time employment with the Leafs in 1955–56 and quickly reached three 20-plus-goal seasons before the calendar turned to 1960.

Solid Leafs teams captured the Stanley Cup in both 1962 and 1963. Duff had the Cup-winning goal on April 22, 1962, in a 2-1 final-game victory over Chicago, erasing the frustration of having missed a good part of the season because of an ankle injury.

The Kirkland Lake, Ontario, native was in his ninth full season with Toronto when he was traded to the Rangers in the blockbuster deal that brought Andy Bathgate to the Leafs. Later in 1964, Duff was dealt to the Montreal Canadiens, a deal that sparked a new chapter in his career. With the Habs, he became a key contributor and helped the team win four Stanley Cups in five seasons, totalling six over the course of his career.

Before his 17-year career ended in 1971, Duff played for the Los Angeles Kings and for former Toronto coach "Punch" Imlach with the Buffalo Sabres. He finished with 283 goals and 572 points in 1,030 NHL games, plus 79 points in 114 Stanley Cup playoff games. He was inducted into the Hall of Fame with the class of 2006.

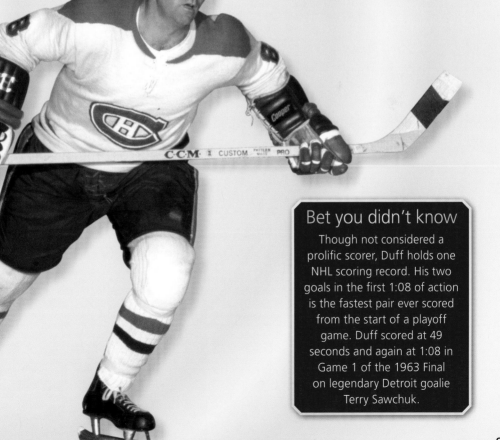

Bet you didn't know

Though not considered a prolific scorer, Duff holds one NHL scoring record. His two goals in the first 1:08 of action is the fastest pair ever scored from the start of a playoff game. Duff scored at 49 seconds and again at 1:08 in Game 1 of the 1963 Final on legendary Detroit goalie Terry Sawchuk.

Aurele Joliat

Compared to some of today's verbal robots, Aurele Joliat was a priceless NHL treasure when it came to the spoken word. "Old-time hockey players like me were the dumbest bunch of athletes in the world," Joliat once said. "We never got paid what we deserved, and most of us didn't have sense enough to save what money we got."

Apart from his colourful insight, Joliat wasn't too bad at hockey, either, authoring a Hall of Fame 16-season career with the Montreal Canadiens that produced three Stanley Cups and 655 games with 270 goals and 460 points.

Known as the "Mighty Atom" and the "Little Giant"—either one was appropriate—Joliat could play it either way, fast or hard. The little left-winger from Ottawa was known to dash up the ice and make a big play. He was also in possession of valuable hockey sense, which made him one of the game's most effective backcheckers—with the ability to break up plays and turn the puck the other way.

Joliat replaced fading star "Newsy" Lalonde on the Canadiens in a controversial trade with a Saskatchewan team in 1922. But Joliat had an immediate impact, helping Montreal claim the Stanley Cup through the challenging series against Vancouver and Calgary in 1924. He later added Cups with Montreal in 1930 and 1931.

In 1934, he won the Hart Trophy when he had 22 goals and 37 points in the 48-game season. Known frequently as Howie Morenz's sidekick, Joliat was also said to be a master at taunting opponents to the point of distraction. When his close friend Morenz died in 1937, Joliat's production declined from 32 to 13 points and he seemed to lose his passion. He retired in 1938.

Bet you didn't know

Later in life, Joliat disputed his retirement circumstances. "Retired hell!" he said. "They fired me when the Montreal Maroons folded and some of their players moved over to the Canadiens. I'm still damn mad about that."

MODERN ERA
LEFT WING

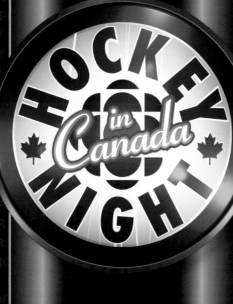

1. Alex Ovechkin
2. Luc Robitaille
3. Brendan Shanahan
4. Michel Goulet
5. Steve Shutt
6. Henrik Zetterberg
7. Bob Gainey
8. Keith Tkachuk
9. Dave Andreychuk
10. Bill Barber

1 Alex Ovechkin

The sky is the limit for Alexander Ovechkin, arguably the most skilled and most exciting player in the National Hockey League. That is not to take anything away from the likes of Sidney Crosby, Evgeni Malkin, or Jonathan Toews—all brilliant entertainers and stars in their own right—it's just that the sum of the Ovechkin parts is a little bit different.

The native of Moscow is a wildly gifted goal scorer who is forever scoring highlight-reel goals—on his belly, off-balance, deking through an entire team, overpowering a defender, with a blistering slapshot...so many different ways. And followed by highlight-reel celebrations to boot.

Selected first overall by the Washington Capitals in 2004, the swift and powerful left winger made his NHL debut in the 2005–06 season when he had 52 goals and 106 points, which was best amongst all rookies and third best in the league. He won the Calder Trophy and was named a rookie and First Team All-Star, the start of a run of those honours. Indeed, he became the first player in 55 years to be named a First Team All-Star in his first two full seasons.

There was a slight drop-off in his numbers in that second season, though not in the electricity of his play. Ovechkin had 46 goals and 92 points, but the most jarring stat was his minus-19 in plus-minus.

In his third season, Ovechkin took his game to another level. He led the league with an amazing 65 goals, the first player to reach that number in a dozen years, since Mario Lemieux. And he was one of just 12 players ever to score that many in a season, 65, also a record for left wingers. He led the league in points with 112, power-play goals

with 22, game-winning goals with 11, and shots with 446. He was also ninth in the league with 220 hits, which completes the sum of the parts.

In so many different ways Ovechkin can punish the opposition. And he does hit to punish. Oh, and that gaudy minus-19 was turned into a handsome plus-28.

While leading the Capitals, who were dead last in November, to the Southeast Division title in April, Ovechkin won the Art Ross Trophy for most points and the "Rocket" Richard Trophy for most goals. He also won the Hart and Pearson Trophies as most valuable player selected by the media and the players, respectively.

Interestingly, no other player has won those four trophies in the same season in the 11 seasons the four have been awarded. Only seven other players have won the big three—Hart, Pearson, and Art Ross—in the 40 years that that hat trick has been available. Wayne Gretzky leads the way, having achieved the triple five times, Lemieux three times, Guy Lafleur twice, Phil Esposito, Jaromir Jagr, Martin St. Louis, and Crosby once each. Ovechkin is keeping some pretty heady company.

He almost pulled off that rare quad again in 2008–09, leading the league with 56 goals to capture the Richard Trophy again, but he just missed winning the scoring title, finishing three points behind Malkin. Ovechkin was still voted the winner of the Hart and Pearson honours, the latter of which is now known as the Ted Lindsay Award.

This past season Ovechkin was third in the league with 50 goals, just one behind Crosby and Steven Stamkos. But he has still managed 50 or more goals in four of his five years in the league, for a total of 269. He added another 59 assists, to finish second

in points with 109, which tied him with Crosby, just three behind Vancouver's Henrik Sedin. Injuries and suspensions, though, limited him to just 72 games, leaving one to wonder how the races might have finished had he played a complete season.

Interestingly, Ovechkin was also plus-45, second best in the league and further evidence of how he has improved his overall game. He also led the league with 368 shots, as the Capitals finished first overall in the NHL for the first time. While Sedin won the Hart Trophy, it was Ovechkin who took the Lindsay, the choice of his peers, for the third straight season. Only Gretzky and Lafleur have accomplished as much.

"Winning the Lindsay means a lot because it's the players who are voting you as the best player," said Ovechkin after his most recent win. "I have the most difficult trophy to get—the players' award. So I am very happy."

A year earlier, though, he was more brazen in his acceptance. "It's important for me," he said. "What I'm doing on the ice, it's working and I don't want to stop. Right now, I'm the best, but next year everyone will be better."

Ovechkin has never been afraid to speak his mind. He exudes confidence, sometimes bordering on arrogance, but he has always backed up his honesty and bold words with play that is just as brazen. A powerful skater, with a great shot and terrific stickhandling skills, Oveckhin often tends to drive right through defenders. And he is just as punishing without the puck. He is the quintessential power forward, often called a runaway train, and once compared to Mark Messier, by no less than Gretzky.

"He has the release and hands that (Mike) Bossy had. He has the quickness that Kurri had, and he has the toughness that Messier had," said Gretzky.

"His future is greatness," Capitals coach Bruce Boudreau once said.

"He is already great," said Capitals general manager George McPhee, suggesting Ovechkin has elements in his game that resemble those of Messier, Gordie Howe, and Rocket Richard. "Time will tell how great he is, but he's been right up there with those guys now, I think."

While he has had success at both the World Junior and World Championship level with Russia, twice winning gold at each, Ovechkin has yet to taste success on the bigger stages—the Olympics and Stanley Cup playoffs. Indeed, these have represented the biggest disappointments of his career. So far.

The 2010 playoffs, on the heels of winning the President's Trophy, really stung as the Capitals were upset by the Montreal Canadiens after leading the series 3–1. The team was the first top seed to blow a lead like that to an eighth seed.

"I don't have words to say," a shaken Ovechkin said afterwards. "Our goal was to win the Stanley Cup. We all played great in the season, but in the playoffs something missed. We just have to concentrate more about playoffs, more about how we have to be in the playoffs."

"Ovi" has already been great in his short NHL career, but the true measure of greatness is leading a team to the big prize. He has openly stated that while he enjoys his individual awards, it is the team awards that he really wants.

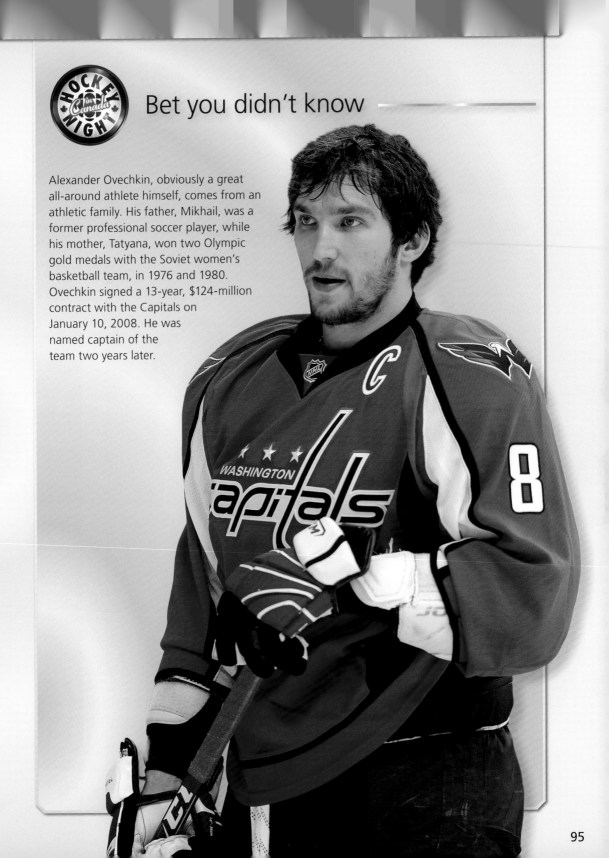

Bet you didn't know

Alexander Ovechkin, obviously a great all-around athlete himself, comes from an athletic family. His father, Mikhail, was a former professional soccer player, while his mother, Tatyana, won two Olympic gold medals with the Soviet women's basketball team, in 1976 and 1980. Ovechkin signed a 13-year, $124-million contract with the Capitals on January 10, 2008. He was named captain of the team two years later.

Luc Robitaille

When he was drafted by the Los Angeles Kings in 1984, the 171st player selected, Luc Robitaille was considered a long shot to make it to the NHL. He returned to junior for a couple of seasons and worked on improving his skills and skating and became a dynamic player, and he was named top junior in Canada in 1986. The next fall, when he arrived at training camp as a 20-year-old, Robitaille was there to stay. He won the Calder Trophy in 1987 after recording 84 points in 79 games.

Robitaille went on to score 53 goals in his second season and in 1992–93 set NHL records for a left winger, scoring 63 goals and 125 points. The points record still stands, while Alex Ovechkin's 65 goals in 2007–08 raised that bar. Robitaille remains the career leader for left wingers in goals (668) and points (1,394). In all, he scored 40 or more goals in all of his first eight seasons in the NHL.

After eight seasons with the Kings, the native of Montreal played in Pittsburgh for a season, then with the New York Rangers for two seasons before returning to Los Angeles for four more seasons. He moved on to Detroit for a couple of years, where he won a Stanley Cup, and returned again to LA to retire as a King.

Robitaille had his sweater number 20 retired by the Kings on January 20, 2007, and is still with the team as president of business operations.

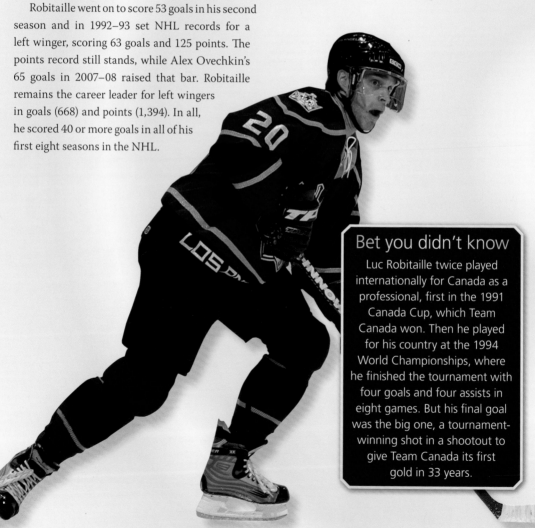

Bet you didn't know

Luc Robitaille twice played internationally for Canada as a professional, first in the 1991 Canada Cup, which Team Canada won. Then he played for his country at the 1994 World Championships, where he finished the tournament with four goals and four assists in eight games. But his final goal was the big one, a tournament-winning shot in a shootout to give Team Canada its first gold in 33 years.

Brendan Shanahan ③

He was the prototypical power forward. Big and strong and fast, Brendan Shanahan was a presence on the ice. Drafted second overall by the New Jersey Devils in 1987, after playing junior with the London Knights, Shanahan started slowly in his first season, largely because of an injury, but he improved dramatically in his second season, scoring 22 goals and earning 50 points. After four seasons with the Devils, Shanahan was signed by St. Louis as a free agent. An arbitrator ruled that the compensation the Blues had to pay for signing Shanahan was defenceman Scott Stevens, who went on to have a stellar career as captain of the Devils.

Shanahan, meantime, blossomed into a big-time scorer with the Blues, twice having 50-plus-goal seasons and earning 102 points in 1993–94. He was caught off guard in 1995 when the Blues traded him to Hartford for defenceman Chris Pronger. Shanahan remained with the Whalers for only one season before he was dealt two games into the next season to Detroit for Paul Coffey, Keith Primeau, and a first-round draft choice. Shanahan scored 46 goals that season and was a key part in the team winning the Stanley Cup.

After three Stanley Cup wins in nine years with the Wings, he signed as a free agent with the Rangers and a few years later returned to New Jersey where he ended his career, announcing his retirement in November 2009. Shanahan finished his career as the league's 11th leading goal scorer with 656. His 1,354 points rank 23rd all-time. Along the way he also amassed 2,489 penalty minutes in his 21 seasons. The Mimico, Ontario, native won Olympic gold with Canada in 2002.

Shanahan was hired by the NHL as vice president of hockey and business development shortly after retiring.

Bet you didn't know

During the NHL lockout, which cancelled the 2004–05 season, Shanahan was credited with calling a two-day meeting, at his expense, that profoundly changed how the game is played. Shanahan assembled 26 people—players, coaches, general managers, owners, agents, television executives—in Toronto in December 2004 to review the game and brainstorm ideas to improve the quality of play. It was dubbed the Shanahan Summit.

Out of those meetings came recommendations for massive changes to the NHL game and different standards for enforcing the rules, as well as the idea of adding a shootout and allowing two-line passes. As much as Shanahan will be remembered for being a great player, he will also be remembered for leading the way for changes to the game.

Michel Goulet

He wasn't necessarily the flashiest player on the ice, but Michel Goulet had a knack for scoring goals. From the time he entered the NHL in 1979 with the Quebec Nordiques, after a season with Birmingham in the WHA, he established himself as a consistent goal scorer.

He recorded 22 goals in his rookie season and proceeded to score 20 or more for 14 consecutive seasons, producing 16 in his final season before retiring in 1994. Late in his final season, in a game in Montreal, Goulet crashed heavily into the boards and suffered a concussion that forced him to call it a career.

"I lost an edge and slammed my head into the bottom of the boards," Goulet said. "I was in a coma for a half hour. For a week in the hospital I had no idea who I was."

Four times he scored more than 50 goals, including 57 in 1982–83 and 56 the following year, and for seven straight seasons produced 40 goals or more. Goulet, who

starred in junior with the Quebec Remparts, played parts of 11 seasons with the Nordiques before he was traded to the Chicago Blackhawks. He played for four more seasons before the injury.

He won the Canada Cup with Team Canada in the 1984 and historic 1987 tournaments and represented the NHL in Rendez-vous '87, a two-game series with the Soviets played in Quebec City. He finished his career with 548 goals and 1,152 points. Exactly one year after he suffered his head injury, Goulet had his number 16 retired by the Nordiques.

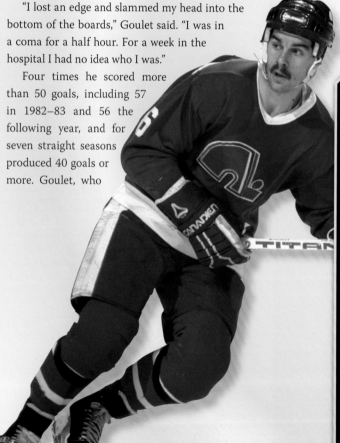

Bet you didn't know

Michel Goulet, a prolific and consistent goal scorer, was inducted into the Hockey Hall of Fame in 1998. Fittingly, he was inducted alongside his former Quebec Nordiques teammate and friend Peter Stastny.

"When you look at your career, the best thing that can ever happen is to be selected to the Hockey Hall of Fame," Goulet said in his Hall biography. "That means that you did something very well in your sport or your job. But just to see Jean Beliveau and Johnny Bucyk and people like that who you've met or played against—just to be part of that was beautiful. The three days (induction weekend) were the most wonderful days I ever had in hockey."

Steve Shutt

He certainly wasn't imposing on the ice, but at the end of the night Steve Shutt could inflict a lot of pain. And he did it by scoring goals aplenty.

Shutt, who grew up in Toronto, had a tremendous junior career with the Marlboros, scoring 144 goals in three seasons while playing on the top line in junior hockey with Bill Harris and Dave Gardner.

Montreal selected Shutt fourth overall in the 1972 draft, in which Harris went number one to the New York Islanders. It took Shutt a couple of seasons to find his way on those dominating Canadiens teams. In his third season he started to emerge, scoring 30 goals playing on a line with Guy Lafleur and Peter Mahovlich. The next season it was 45 goals and the following season, 1976–77, it was 60 goals with his linemates Lafleur and Jacques Lemaire.

The 60 goals were a record for left wingers at the time, a mark ultimately surpassed by Luc Robitaille with 63 and later still by Alex Ovechkin with 65. That Canadiens team had a best-ever 60-8-12 season en route to another Stanley Cup.

Shutt strung together nine straight seasons with 30 or more goals and played on five championship teams in Montreal. In his 13th season with the Habs he was dealt to Los Angeles, where he finished the season with the Kings and retired. He had no interest in playing for anyone but Montreal. Shutt finished his career with 424 goals and 817 points and was inducted into the Hockey Hall of Fame in 1993.

Bet you didn't know

Legendary Canadiens general manager Sam Pollock was a shrewd trader. He was forever dealing aging players and Band-Aid fixes to expansion teams for high draft picks. He knew he had to keep replenishing his talent supply.

On June 11, 1968, Pollock traded a good goaltender in Gerry Desjardins to the Los Angeles Kings in exchange for the Kings' first selections in 1969 and 1972. The Canadiens ultimately traded away the 1969 pick but kept the 1972 pick and used it to select Steve Shutt fourth overall. That year, the first two picks belonged to the expansion New York Islanders and Atlanta Flames, who took Bill Harris and Jacques Richard, respectively. With the third pick, Vancouver selected Don Lever. The Canadiens had three picks in the top eight that year, taking goaltender Michel Larocque sixth and Shutt's junior centre Dave Gardner eighth.

Henrik Zetterberg

His career is still very much a work in progress, but what Henrik Zetterberg has accomplished already is very impressive.

Once described by Wayne Gretzky as being the most underrated player in the game, people have now taken notice of how well Zetterberg plays. Selected 210th overall in the 1999 Entry Draft by Detroit, the native of Njurunda, Sweden, didn't join the Red Wings until the 2002–03 season, after being named Sweden's top player the previous year.

In that first year, he produced 22 goals and 44 points to lead all rookies, although he was the runner-up for the Calder Trophy. Interestingly he was named top rookie by *The Sporting News*, which had polled players.

Zetterberg played that season on a line with Pavel Datsyuk, who is still his centre, and an aging Brett Hull, who called the line "two kids and an old goat."

Two seasons later, Zetterberg stepped up his play and produced 39 goals and 85 points. A back injury limited him to 33 goals the following season, but he bounced back with 43 the year after that. The Wings won the Stanley Cup that year and Zetterberg was awarded the Conn Smythe Trophy. He strung together four straight 30-goal plus seasons before falling back to 23 in 2009–10.

Zetterberg is regarded for his great speed and puckhandling skills and his quick release.

Bet you didn't know

As good as he is offensively, Henrik Zetterberg is also responsible defensively and was a finalist for the Selke Trophy in 2008, finishing third behind teammate Pavel Datsyuk and John Madden. That season, he scored 43 goals in the regular season and was plus-30. He added another 13 goals and 27 points to lead all playoff scorers as the Red Wings beat the Pittsburgh Penguins to win the Stanley Cup.

Bob Gainey

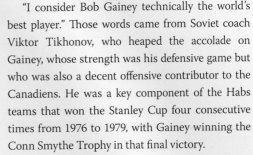

In 1977, the NHL decided it was to going introduce a new award to recognize the best defensive forward in the game. It was called the Selke Trophy, after the late manager of the Maple Leafs and Canadiens, but for a while it could have been called the Bob Gainey Trophy.

Indeed, the great Canadiens winger won the trophy the first four years it was presented, from 1978 through 1981, which happened to be the year Gainey received the highest praise ever.

"I consider Bob Gainey technically the world's best player." Those words came from Soviet coach Viktor Tikhonov, who heaped the accolade on Gainey, whose strength was his defensive game but who was also a decent offensive contributor to the Canadiens. He was a key component of the Habs teams that won the Stanley Cup four consecutive times from 1976 to 1979, with Gainey winning the Conn Smythe Trophy in that final victory.

Gainey won a fifth Stanley Cup, as captain, in 1986. Not bad for a player many scouts believed wasn't a can't-miss pro. At best, scouts doubted Gainey was a high first-round pick. But Habs general manager Sam Pollock, a genius at the draft table, knew otherwise and took Gainey eighth overall from the Peterborough Petes, where he played under Roger Neilson, himself a great defensive coach.

Ironically, Gainey's best year offensively was 1981, the same year he won his final Selke Trophy. The Peterborough, Ontario, native had 23 goals and 24 assists that season and was named captain for the following season.

A great leader, Gainey played on two Canada Cup teams, winning in 1976 and losing to the Soviets in 1981. He retired after 16 seasons with the Canadiens and later became the coach and, later still, general manager with the Minnesota North Stars, moving with the franchise to Dallas, where he built a powerhouse team that won the Stanley Cup in 1999.

Bet you didn't know

After Bob Gainey retired from the Montreal Canadiens in 1989 he didn't retire from hockey—just the Habs and the NHL. Gainey signed a one-year contract as player-coach with the Epinal Squirrels in France. As much as Gainey wanted a new experience for his family, it was also part of the transition process into a management position.

Keith Tkachuk

Off the ice Keith Tkachuk was never shy about sharing his opinion or being brutally honest about how he felt. He could be brutal as well—as in brutally tough to play against.

After a humble beginning with the Winnipeg Jets, who drafted him 19th overall in 1990, Tkachuk turned into a premier power forward and will be remembered as one of the best U.S.-born players ever. "He came in raw and just evolved into a great player," said former Jets teammate Ed Olczyk. "He was the prototypical power forward. He could score. He could hit. He wasn't afraid to run you into the ditch. He was a great pro. He's one of the greatest American-born players to play the game."

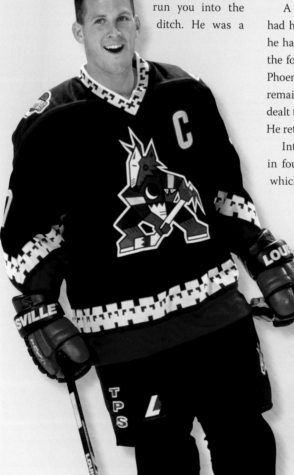

Ultimately, it was all the bumps and bruises and the physical toll from playing the style he did that prompted Tkachuk to retire after the 2009–10 season, his 19th in the NHL. He finished his career with the St. Louis Blues, his second stint with that team, having played 1,201 games in all.

The Melrose, Massachusetts, native scored 538 goals and 1,065 points and sat in the penalty box for a whopping 2,219 penalty minutes. He is just the fourth player in NHL history with 1,000 points and at least 2,200 penalty minutes.

A five-time All-Star Team selection, Tkachuk had his best season statistically in 1995–96, when he had 50 goals and 98 points. He scored 52 goals the following season when the franchise moved to Phoenix. He was traded to the Blues in 2001 and remained there for another five seasons before being dealt to the Atlanta Thrashers at the trade deadline. He returned to the Blues the following season.

Internationally, he represented the United States in four Olympics, including the 2002 Games, in which he won a silver medal.

Bet you didn't know

At one point early in his career, Keith Tkachuk was one of the highest-paid players in the NHL. In 1995, while he was with the Winnipeg Jets, he became a free agent and received a five-year, $17.2-million offer sheet from the Chicago Blackhawks. Winnipeg decided to match the offer, which included a $6-million salary in the first year, making Tkachuk the third-highest player in the league behind Wayne Gretzky and Mark Messier.

Dave Andreychuk ⑨

Good things come to those who wait, and so it was with Dave Andreychuk. In his 22nd season in the NHL, the right-hand shot who mostly played left wing finally won his first Stanley Cup, with the Tampa Lightning, beating the Calgary Flames in seven games before the lights went out and the NHL had it's year-long lockout. (Andreychuk would play one more season with the Lightning before retiring.)

It was quite a wait for Andreychuk, who played with six different teams over his 23-season career. When he finally got to hoist the Stanley Cup high above his head, he had tied Raymond Bourque for the most years without winning the championship, and at 40 years and seven months of age, he was the oldest player to play in his first Finals game. But the wait was worth it.

"To win it in what I knew was pretty much my last shot, and to win it as a captain for a team that brought me in to help them become a better team, was just such a satisfying moment," he said.

Andreychuk, a native of Hamilton, Ontario, was selected in the first round, 16th overall, by the Buffalo Sabres in the 1982 Entry Draft. He had 11 solid seasons there before being dealt to the Maple Leafs where, playing alongside Doug Gilmour, he took his game to another level, scoring 54 goals (29 in Buffalo, 25 in Toronto) in 1993, and 53 goals and 99 points with the Leafs the following season.

Andreychuk had a terrific touch around the net. He often parked himself outside the crease and had great hand-eye coordination to deflect the puck. When the Leafs started a rebuild, they dealt Andreychuk to New Jersey. He later signed with Boston as a free agent and was traded to Colorado along with Bourque. The Avs didn't win in 2000, but Bourque stayed on for another year and finally did win, while Andreychuk returned to Buffalo for a season then signed with the Lightning as a free agent.

He finished his career having played 1,639 games, fifth most in league history, with 640 goals and 1,338 points.

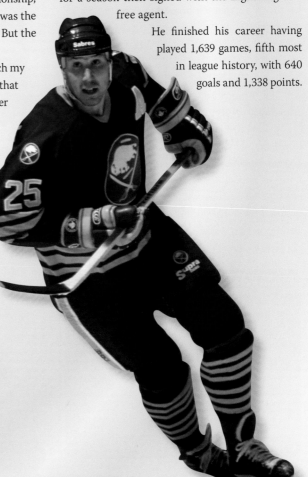

Bet you didn't know

Over his 23-year career, Dave Andreychuk played with six different teams and wore six different numbers, but his favourite was 23 because his favourite player was former Montreal Canadiens star Bob Gainey. "I always liked his style; a hard worker, smart, a great leader."

Bill Barber

He was a centre in junior hockey, selected seventh overall, and was playing down the middle when he joined the Philadelphia Flyers in 1972. But a decision by the late Fred Shero, who was coach of the Flyers, had a profound impact on the career of Bill Barber.

Rather than have him languish as a fourth-line centre and see limited ice time, Shero decided to move Barber to the left wing, where he immediately hit if off with centre Bobby Clarke and Reggie Leach on right wing.

In his first season, Barber scored 30 goals and added 34 assists. It was the start of four straight 30-plus goal seasons, with Barber scoring 50 goals in that fourth season. Along the way, in 1974 and 1975, the Flyers became the first expansion team to win the Stanley Cup. His best season statistically was 1975–76 when he scored those 50 goals and added 62 assists for the Broad Street Bullies. After dipping to 20 goals the following season he bounced back with five consecutive seasons in which he had more than 30 goals, including four years of at least 40.

As good as Barber was as a goal scorer, he was often accused by opponents of being a first-rate diver. He played a dozen seasons with the Flyers, finishing with 420 goals and 883 points. He also played for the winning Canadian team in the 1976 Canada Cup and for the NHL in the 1979 Challenge Cup against the Soviet Union. He was inducted into the Hockey Hall of Fame in 1990.

Bet you didn't know

When he retired in 1984, Bill Barber got into coaching, first with the Hershey Bears and later with the Philadelphia Phantoms, whom he helped lead to the 1998 Calder Cup championship in the AHL. After a stint as an assistant coach in 2000, Barber became head coach of the Flyers in the 2000–01 season, winning the Jack Adams Award. He held the job for one more season before being replaced by Ken Hitchcock.

ORIGINAL SIX

GOALIE

1. Terry Sawchuk
2. Jacques Plante
3. Glenn Hall
4. Johnny Bower
5. Walter "Turk" Broda
6. Georges Vezina
7. Bill Durnan
8. George Hainsworth
9. Lorne "Gump" Worsley
10. Frank Brimsek

① Terry Sawchuk

He was one of the greatest goaltenders of all time, and one of the most tortured. His nickname was "Butch," but his teammates usually called him "Uke" or "Ukey" because he was of Ukrainian descent.

Regardless, virtually everyone called Terry Sawchuk the best goaltender in the game. "The Uke was the best goalie I ever saw," the legendary Gordie Howe once told hockey reporter Frank Orr. "He was everything that a goalie should be. Terry simply hated to give up goals, and it bothered him when he did. If many other goalies got bombed in the game, they went out and got bombed themselves and forgot about it. Not the Uke. He would brood about a loss or a bad goal for days. He was such a wreck from injuries and parts of his body just wearing out. But through it all he could sure stop the puck."

Sawchuk began playing goal in his hometown of Winnipeg at the age of 10. When the goalie on his team unexpectedly switched to another team, Sawchuk was put in because he had the equipment. It belonged to his older brother, Mike, who had died at the age of 17 because of a heart ailment.

"My big brother's goalie pads were the first ones I ever used," Sawchuk told a reporter. "Our uncle gave them to him originally. My brother had a heart murmur and died when he was 17. I couldn't believe it when it happened. I missed him for a long time afterwards. I used to try them on once in a while. I'd played around the rinks with them, too. The day they put me in the net I had a good game. I've stayed there since."

He was playing junior hockey by the age of 15 for a team sponsored by Chicago. On his father's advice, Sawchuk wouldn't sign to become the Black Hawks' property. Instead he signed with the Red Wings, who assigned him to their Galt, Ontario, junior farm team.

In addition to being a great goaltender, Sawchuk was also an accomplished baseball player, a power-hitting first baseman. He was offered a tryout contract by the St. Louis Cardinals. While playing with the Red Wings' farm team in Indianapolis, he was offered a contract by the Cleveland Indians, which he accepted, though he later wisely decided to focus on hockey.

The first shot Sawchuk faced as a professional may have been a goal, but there weren't many more after that. Indeed, the Winnipeg native broke in full time with the Red Wings in 1950–51, played every game that season, led the league in wins (44) and shutouts (11), and had a crisp 1.99 goals-against average. He missed winning the Vezina Trophy, as the NHL's best goaltender, by one goal, but he did win the Calder Trophy as the top rookie. In fact, he was the first player and the only goalie to be named top rookie in three different professional leagues.

The next season Sawchuk increased his shutouts to an even dozen, had the same number of wins and lowered his goals-against average to 1.90. Those back-to-back 44-win seasons stood as a record for more than 20 years. In his first five seasons with the Red Wings, Sawchuk led the team to three Stanley Cup championships (1952, 1954, and 1955). He also won the Vezina Trophy three times (1952, 1953, and 1955), was three times a First Team All-Star and was named to the Second Team the other two seasons. Before his career was over, Sawchuk won another Vezina and Stanley Cup with the Toronto Maple Leafs.

During the 1952 playoffs, he tied a playoff record with four shutouts. He did it in just eight games, as the Red Wings swept their way to a Stanley Cup win.

"He was the greatest angles goalie of all time," said former Montreal Canadiens great "Boom Boom" Geoffrion.

Sawchuk was admired for his incredible reflexes and quick hands. He was one of the first goaltenders to play in a deep crouch, something that ultimately led to severe back problems and surgery.

"In action, he was the most acrobatic goaltender of his time," wrote sportswriter Trent Frayne. "He didn't move so much as he exploded into a desperate release of energy—down the glove, up the arm, over the stick, up the leg pad. He sometimes seemed a human pinwheel. He played the whole game in pent-up tension, shouting at his teammates, crouching, straightening, diving, scrambling, his pale face drawn and tense."

After that remarkable five-year start, in which he amassed an incredible 56 shutouts and his goals-against average was below 2.00, Sawchuk was surprisingly included in a nine-player trade with the Boston Bruins. The Red Wings feared his play was being affected by nerves, and believed the young Glenn Hall had a more promising future.

"We'd been negotiating a trade with Detroit over several players and they knew we wanted a goalkeeper," Bruins general manager Lynn Patrick said at the time. "But no goaltender's name had been mentioned...when we learned that the mysterious goalkeeper was Terry, we were dumbfounded."

Sawchuk's stay with Boston was not long, however. Midway through his second season, after recovering from a bout of mononucleosis and again playing well, Sawchuk announced he was retiring at the age of 27, admitting his nerves were frayed. "I can't eat or sleep," he said. "I'm getting out of the game."

The Red Wings ultimately brought him back, sending Hall to Chicago and trading Johnny Bucyk to Boston to get Sawchuk's rights. He remained in Detroit for seven more seasons before they left him unprotected in the 1964 intra-league draft. Sawchuk was claimed by the Maple Leafs, with whom he played three seasons and was brilliant in the 1967 playoffs.

There is a famous story, retold by the late Punch Imlach in his book *Hockey is a Battle*, about

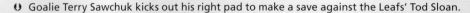

⟳ Goalie Terry Sawchuk kicks out his right pad to make a save against the Leafs' Tod Sloan.

Sawchuk earlier that spring. Sawchuk had been given a night off in the Leafs' series with the Black Hawks, but had to be put in during the second period. Minutes after he entered the game, he was felled by a booming slap shot off the stick of Bobby Hull. As the story goes, when the trainer got to Sawchuk, he asked him if he was okay.

"I stopped it, didn't I?" Sawchuk replied.

Sawchuk was great in the final against Montreal, too, taking over from an ailing Johnny Bower to lead Toronto to its last Stanley Cup win. "That's the way I'd like to go out," Sawchuk told a reporter after the final game. "In style."

Sawchuk didn't retire, though, and was claimed in the expansion draft that summer by the Los Angeles Kings. He played a season there, another in Detroit, and one more with the New York Rangers at the age of 40. It was following that final season with the Rangers that Sawchuk died, days after undergoing surgery for internal injuries he accidentally suffered during a playful scuffle with friend and teammate Ron Stewart.

For years, Sawchuk held the NHL record for career shutouts (103), which was broken in 2010 by Martin Brodeur, and games played (971), passed by Patrick Roy and Brodeur. He finished with 447 wins, still fifth best all-time.

As great as Sawchuk was on the ice, though, he was reportedly not a happy man. He was often described as moody and sullen. "Most of the time he was a morose loner," wrote the late Jim Proudfoot in *The Toronto Star*.

"I was his roommate on the road for many years and I never did quite figure the Uke out," defenceman Marcel Pronovost told Orr. "When we woke up in the morning, I would say good morning to him in both French and English. If he answered I knew we would talk at least a little that day. But if he didn't reply, which was most of the days, we didn't speak the entire day."

Sawchuk was inducted in the Hockey Hall of Fame in 1971.

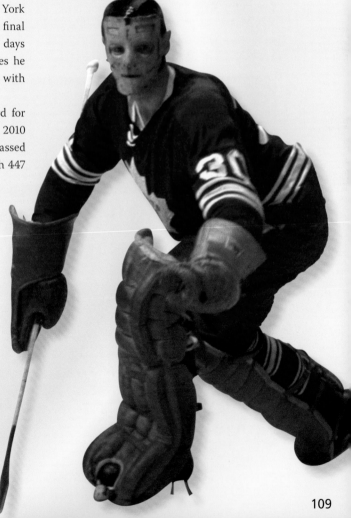

Bet you didn't know

Sawchuk was once described by his son, Jerry, as being a "medical freak." He had numerous surgeries, had more than 400 stitches in his face, and had severed tendons in his hand and fingers which left him unable to make a fist. Sawchuk had a chronic bad back and stoop from crouching for so many years, which ultimately required surgery, and he had countless broken bones. When he was 12, he suffered a broken right arm playing football and the arm wound up being two inches shorter than his left. He almost lost an eye playing in a game on his 18th birthday when he was clipped by a stick.

All of which prompted him to develop a curious hobby. "I've been collecting all of the parts they take out of me," Sawchuk once told the *Toronto Telegram*. "I have one bottle for the teeth I've lost, another for the bone chips and another for my appendix. I had them specially pickled to add to the collection. I know it sounds odd, but what's the difference between that and collecting stamps or old coins? Not many people have the chance to get the collection I have of old pieces of me."

In the 1964 playoffs, Sawchuk was hospitalized for a pinched nerve in his shoulder. He was released on game nights to play, and would then return to the hospital.

Jacques Plante

Jacques Plante was not only a great goaltender, he was also an innovator at his position. Best known for being the first goalie to regularly wear a mask in NHL games, Plante was also known for developing and refining the art of puck handling. He was one of a very few who played the puck outside the crease and he became the first to regularly play the puck behind the net. Plante was also the first to signal icing calls to his defencemen.

Considered eccentric off the ice, Plante was brilliant on it. He personified the stand-up style goaltending of the time, cutting down his angles, remaining square to the shooter. Indeed, Plante was not only a student of his position but of the game.

He challenged legendary Montreal coach "Toe" Blake about wearing a mask in an actual game— Blake was against the idea—and finally did don the mask on the night of November 1, 1959, after he had been struck in the face with a puck. While Blake wasn't pleased, it was the only way Plante would return to the goal, and he did so with great success, leading the Habs to an 11-game unbeaten streak.

Plante had a distinguished career with Montreal, winning the Stanley Cup six times. He was also a key to the Habs team that won the Cup in five consecutive seasons, while he won the Vezina Trophy those same five years and seven times in all.

Plante moved on from Montreal to play two seasons with the New York Rangers before retiring for a couple of years. He returned to the NHL to join the expansion St. Louis Blues, leading them to two Stanley Cup finals. He shared a final Vezina Trophy with the legendary Glenn Hall in 1969. Plante ended his NHL career with Boston before playing a final season with Edmonton in the WHA.

Plante was inducted in the Hockey Hall of Fame in 1978.

Bet you didn't know

In an era of train travel, most players played cards to pass the time, but Plante read books and enjoyed knitting. He also brought some team owners to their knees in embarrassment, rightly pointing out at his own press conference that the goal nets were two inches lower in New York, Boston, and Chicago than they were in Montreal, Toronto, and Detroit. He was ridiculed for this observation until the nets were measured in all buildings and Plante was found to be correct. Plante also regularly lobbied for a two-goalie system in an era when most teams employed only one.

Glenn Hall

His nickname was "Mr. Goalie," which tells you just how good Glenn Hall was in his day. They also could have called him the "Iron Man." Hall, who played 18 seasons in the NHL with Detroit, Chicago, and St. Louis, started an incredible 502 consecutive regular-season games and another 50 straight playoff games between 1955 and 1962. He played through injuries and pain, and ultimately the streak ended because of back issues.

In his rookie season in 1956, Hall played all 70 games and finished with a 2.10 goals-against average, with a dozen shutouts, earning him the Calder Trophy as top rookie. Hall was just as good the next season, but he was blamed for a playoff loss to Boston and was included in the

controversial Ted Lindsay trade to Chicago. It was believed the motivation behind moving Lindsay was his involvement in trying to create a players' union, and his questioning of what the owners were doing with the players' pension money.

Hall had a stellar career with the Black Hawks, winning the Stanley Cup in 1961. He was a First Team All-Star seven times and a Second Team All-Star four times. All but one of those All-Star selections came at a time when there were just six teams in the NHL, and when other legends played goal—a heady accomplishment indeed. Hall also won the Vezina Trophy three times and the Conn Smythe Trophy once, as most valuable player in the playoffs in a losing cause with St. Louis in 1968.

Hall was something of an innovator in the crease himself, albeit the exact opposite of a Jacques Plante. Hall was one of the first to play the "butterfly" style, dropping to his knees, pads spread. It was unorthodox at times, but for Hall it was incredibly effective.

Hall played 906 NHL games, with 407 wins and an excellent 2.49 goals-against average and 84 shutouts, third best all-time. He was inducted into the Hockey Hall of Fame in 1975.

Bet you didn't know

By his own count Hall amassed some 300 stitches on his face, mostly around his mouth and under his eyes, but he didn't don a mask until he teamed with Jacques Plante in St. Louis at the end of his career.

This is even more remarkable because, like a lot of goaltenders of his era, Hall had a tendency to get physically ill before games because of nerves and fears. Several times, in fact, Hall would retire and miss training camp. He would say he was busy painting the barn on his farm but would eventually return to play in the regular season.

Johnny Bower

As the old line goes, Johnny Bower was an overnight success—a dozen years or so in the making. Perhaps that is what endeared Bower so much to Toronto Maple Leafs fans—that and the fact he helped lead the Leafs to three consecutive Stanley Cup wins from 1962–1964. He also contributed to the very last Cup the Leafs won, in 1967, with the famous "Over the Hill Gang."

Bower, at the time, was a young 42.

Bower's story is one of bravery and perseverance. He played a dozen seasons in the AHL, including eight with the Cleveland Barons, and was named the league's top player and goaltender three times before he finally earned full-time employment in the NHL with the Leafs, in 1958.

Known as "The China Wall" (because, his teammates joked, he was as old as that great construction) Bower twice won the Vezina Trophy and was a First-Team All-Star in 1961. He played a dozen NHL seasons with the Leafs

before retiring in 1970 and was regarded for his work ethic and dedication as well as his artful poke check. Bower was fearless, willingly lunging towards an opposing forward to poke the puck off his stick. He suffered numerous cuts to his face and mouth and had almost all his teeth dislodged, either by shots to the face, or even skates when he was poking away the puck.

Bower was inducted to the Hockey Hall of Fame in 1976 and his name and number have been honoured with a banner by the Leafs at the Air Canada Centre.

Bet you didn't know

Bower routinely lied about his age, first when he joined the military as a teenager and later throughout his AHL and NHL career when goalies were often considered to be on the downside of their careers by age 30. Best guess estimates were that Bower was already 34 when the Leafs signed him and according to records that are thought to be authentic, he won that 1967 Cup at age 42, the oldest goalie in the league at the time. He retired four months past his 45th birthday.

Walter "Turk" Broda

Walter "Turk" Broda was famous not just for his nickname (which had nothing to do with his nationality; in fact, he was of Polish descent), but because he was one of the unbeatable goaltenders of his era.

"Toe Blake couldn't beat him, I couldn't beat him, none of the Canadiens could," said the legendary Maurice "Rocket" Richard after one of the many Stanley Cup final series in which Toronto and Broda beat Montreal.

Broda was in net for the historic Leafs comeback from being down three games to none in the 1942 Stanley Cup final against Detroit. That kind of a comeback has happened just three times in the history of the playoffs and Broda was the reason it happened for the Leafs.

He played his entire career at Maple Leaf Gardens, 14 seasons in all, and it might have been more had he not taken off two seasons to commit to the efforts in the Second World War (a commitment that saw him play hockey in England rather than participate in combat).

In total, Broda won the Stanley Cup five times with the Leafs, including three in a row from 1947 to 1949. He won the Vezina Trophy twice and was twice a First Team All-Star. He was inducted into the Hall of Fame in 1967 and is perhaps best known for the legendary 1951 final versus Montreal in which every game went to overtime, earning him both the ire and admiration of "The Rocket."

⊃ Goalie Turk Broda get a hug from his boss, Leafs' owner Conn Smythe.

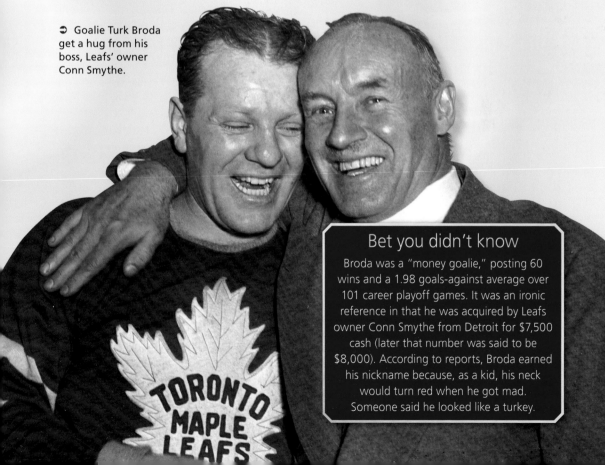

Bet you didn't know

Broda was a "money goalie," posting 60 wins and a 1.98 goals-against average over 101 career playoff games. It was an ironic reference in that he was acquired by Leafs owner Conn Smythe from Detroit for $7,500 cash (later that number was said to be $8,000). According to reports, Broda earned his nickname because, as a kid, his neck would turn red when he got mad. Someone said he looked like a turkey.

Georges Vezina

It's impossible to say with clarity how good Georges Vezina was, or even how he would compare to the best in the game today. Statistics aren't a true measure because hockey was obviously a vastly different game back in the early 1900s.

When Vezina entered the National Hockey Association for the 1910–11 season there was no videotape to document style and goalies were forbidden from falling down to the ice, at least by design. That rule led to Vezina developing what later came to be known as the "stand-up" style.

Longtime watchers of that era said the Montreal netminder virtually perfected the stand-up style and regularly made as many saves with his stick as he did with his gloves. During his first two seasons in the league he led in goals-against average. In the 1913–14 season, he led the Canadiens to first place overall. Two seasons later he led the Canadiens to their first Stanley Cup win in franchise history. Vezina was the first NHL goalie to record a shutout (during the league's inaugural 1917–18 season). He won two Cups with the Canadiens (the second in 1924) and led the league in goals-against average (2.00) in 1923–24 and 1924–25.

Vezina, who was nicknamed the "Chicoutimi Cucumber" for his calm demeanour on the ice, was inducted to the Hockey Hall of Fame in 1945,

Bet you didn't know

Vezina's name was applied to the trophy recognizing the best goaltender in the NHL during the regular season in part for how he played, but also to maintain the memory of him after he died at an early age. Early in the 1925–26 season, he left a game because he was bleeding from the mouth. He collapsed in the dressing room and later returned, only to collapse again. Shortly thereafter, Vezina, at the age of 39, died of tuberculosis. Ownership of the Canadiens proposed a trophy in his honour starting with the 1926–27 season and the Vezina Trophy, annually awarded to the league's top goaltender (later goaltenders) was born.

Bill Durnan

Like a lot of goalies of his era, Durnan bided his time before making it to the NHL. But like so many before him, once he arrived, at age 27, he made an impact.

Durnan was a rarity in that he was ambidextrous, and that particular talent—he was able to handle his stick well in either hand and to catch with either hand—served him very well, indeed. In his rookie season with the Montreal Canadiens, he posted a 38-5-7 record and appeared in every game (50). He also won his first of two Stanley Cups, the Vezina Trophy, and a berth on the league's First All-Star Team.

Durnan entered the NHL during the war years (1943), but the Canadiens were better for his arrival—even though they still had the famed "Punch Line" intact with "Toe" Blake, Elmer Lach, and Maurice "The Rocket" Richard. Durnan was a stand-up netminder but his style, in part because of his athletic ability, was difficult for opposing shooters to solve.

He was the first goalie to win four consecutive Vezina Trophies (1944–47). He was also a First Team All-Star in each of those seasons. In 1949, he established a shutout streak of 309 minutes and 21 seconds, a record that stood until Brian Boucher topped the mark with the Phoenix Coyotes in 2004. In all, Durnan won the Vezina Trophy six times and earned six First Team All-Star designations.

Bet you didn't know

Durnan served as co-captain of the Canadiens, the last goalie to wear the captain's "C". The Vancouver Canucks gave the honour to Roberto Luongo in 2009, but NHL rules prohibit him wearing the letter. Durnan also ended his career, at age 34, during a playoff series with the New York Rangers, retiring with his team down three games to one in the series. He cited nerves as the reason he quit. He was inducted into the Hockey Hall of Fame in 1964 and died in 1972 at the age of 56. The only year Durnan didn't win the Vezina was when Toronto's Turk Broda took it in 1947–48.

⑧ George Hainsworth

If Georges Vezina set the bar early, George Hainsworth pushed it higher. He was the winner of the Vezina Trophy the first three seasons after it was established, entering the NHL with the Montreal Canadiens after some early years in the Western Hockey League. He also played with the Toronto Maple Leafs later in his career.

Hainsworth won the Vezina in 1927 and the following two seasons and by the end of the 1928–29 season he set the all-time record for shutouts in a season (22) and posted a goals-against average of 0.92 while playing 44 games. The following season Hainsworth set an NHL record that still stands, going 270 minutes and 8 seconds without allowing a goal in the playoffs for the Canadiens. He won Cups with the Canadiens that season and again in 1931.

Hainsworth posted 94 NHL shutouts, third on the all-time list behind legends Martin Brodeur and Terry Sawchuk. His career goals against average was an astounding 1.93.

Bet you didn't know

Hainsworth was a pioneer in the field of athlete-turned-broadcaster, becoming something of a regular on Toronto's Hot Stove broadcasts after his career ended. He recorded 10 shutouts in the old Western Hockey League when that was a pro league, for a time giving him one more than Terry Sawchuk, who was acknowledged as the NHL shutout king until Martin Brodeur broke his mark. Hainsworth was elected to the Hockey Hall of Fame in 1961.

Lorne "Gump" Worsley

9

Lorne John "Gump" Worsley could sum up his hockey career in one word: winner.

En route to the NHL he played in five different leagues and took top honours in all of them. When he made it to the NHL at age 24 with the New York Rangers, he won the Calder Trophy as rookie of the year, yet incredibly was sent back to the minors for another season of seasoning.

Worsley didn't have legendary win totals and made the playoffs in only four of his 10 seasons with the Rangers, but the Rangers were a very poor team in Worsley's time. In fact, the consensus was that he was the only reason they made the post-season those four times, and he was arguably the team's best player in most of the other seasons as well.

Worsley also played seven years with the Montreal Canadiens and excelled, winning the Stanley Cup four times with the Habs. A white-knuckle flyer, Worsley retired in 1969 but was convinced, in part because of reduced travel and in part because of performance bonuses, to return later that season by the Minnesota North Stars.

Worsley was as good with a quip as he was with a stick or glove. He once famously answered "My own" when asked which team gave him the most trouble in the NHL. It was a stinging indictment of the Rangers, but it was done with good humour, a trademark of Worsley's long career.

Worsley shared in two Vezina trophies with three other NHL legends, Jacques Plante, Charlie Hodge, and Rogie Vachon. He played 21 years in the NHL, retired for the last time at age 44, and was elected to the Hockey Hall of Fame in 1980.

Bet you didn't know

"Gump" Worsley was in the nets as the goalie of record when Bobby Hull, the "Golden Jet," scored his 500th NHL goal. His nickname "Gump" came from a childhood friend. When he reached the NHL and filled out a form asking for his nickname, he used "Gump" and it became a part of his legacy from that day forward. It was an offshoot of Andy Gump, a famous cartoon strip character during Worsley's youth. No relation to Forrest Gump.

Frank Brimsek

Before Terry Sawchuk had the moniker "Mr. Zero," the honour belonged to Frank Brimsek, one of the greatest American-born goaltenders of all time. In his 10 years in the NHL, the native of Minnesota registered 40 shutouts and won 252 regular-season games. Brimsek led all goaltenders in shutouts, goals-against average, and wins twice in his career and led the Boston Bruins to two Stanley Cup wins, the first in 1939 and again in 1941.

He won the Calder Trophy in his rookie season, largely on the strength of an incredible 33 wins and 10 shutouts and a stop-all-shots style that stymied the best shooters of his era. Brimsek won two Vezina Trophies, and he might have won more but, like a lot of players, he also saw military service during the Second World War. He played three seasons with the Bruins after returning to civilian life and was eventually sold to the Chicago Black Hawks. Just before that transaction he finished second to Buddy O'Connor of the New York Rangers for the Hart Trophy, a rare honour for a goaltender.

Brimsek played all 70 games in his one season with the Black Hawks before retiring with nine 20-win seasons to his credit.

Bet you didn't know

Brimsek was elected to the Hockey Hall of Fame in 1966 and was a member of the inaugural class of the United States Hockey Hall of Fame in his native Eveleth, Minnesota. To this day, an annual trophy celebrating his name is given to the top goaltender in Minnesota high school hockey.

MODERN ERA

GOALIE

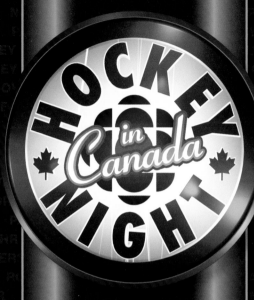

1. **MARTIN BRODEUR**
2. **PATRICK ROY**
3. **DOMINIK HASEK**
4. **GRANT FUHR**
5. **KEN DRYDEN**
6. **BERNIE PARENT**
7. **BILLY SMITH**
8. **TONY ESPOSITO**
9. **GERRY CHEEVERS**
10. **ED BELFOUR**

Martin Brodeur

When he was a youngster, a seven- or eight-year-old growing up in Montreal, Martin Brodeur had a big decision to make. His minor hockey coach asked him if he wanted to continue playing forward or would he play the season in goal?

Brodeur has said he isn't sure why he made the choice he did—perhaps it was because his father had played the position himself; perhaps it was because he had filled in at a tournament the previous season—but Brodeur opted to play goal, and the rest, as they say, is history.

On the day that decision was made, arguably the greatest goaltender in NHL history was born. Indeed, if the true measure of greatness is in the statistics, then it is hard to say Brodeur is anything but the best. Consider the numbers. Brodeur, who was selected 20th overall in the 1990 Entry Draft and completed his 17th season with the New Jersey Devils in 2009–10, leads all goaltenders in wins with 602 (and counting), having surpassed his idol Patrick Roy (551) a season earlier.

Brodeur, at the age of 37, also became the NHL's all-time shutout leader, eclipsing a record by the late Terry Sawchuk that few ever thought would be broken. For more than 40 years, Sawchuk was the runaway leader with 103 career regular-season shutouts, but on December 23, 2009, Brodeur broke the record with a 4-0 shutout of Sidney Crosby and the Penguins in Pittsburgh.

"Terry Sawchuk set a shutout record that stood for more than 45 years and withstood the challenge of more than 500 goaltenders who have played in the National Hockey League since then," NHL commissioner Gary Bettman said that night. "By surpassing that record, Martin Brodeur reached yet another level of goaltending supremacy."

Brodeur registered nine shutouts in 2009–10 to raise his career total to an incredible 110. He is tied with Roy with 23 playoff shutouts. Brodeur is also the all-time leader in games played with 1,076, again passing Roy for top spot. That includes playing more than 70 games in a season a dozen times, including 10 straight seasons. Talk about durability and athleticism.

"It tells you how good this guy has been," said former Devils coach Jacques Lemaire. "He's getting older and he's still in the net mostly every game and doing well."

Brodeur owns the record for most 30-plus win seasons with 13, and of that total, he has won more than 40 games eight different times. No other goalie has done that. He is also the all-time minutes-played leader and sports a career goals-against average of 2.21. Beyond that, he has won the Stanley Cup three times and has missed the playoffs just once in his career. In his first Cup win, a sweep of the Detroit Red Wings in 1995, he allowed just seven goals.

He has also won the William Jennings Trophy five times, the Vezina Trophy four times, the Calder Trophy, and he has twice won Olympic gold. Oh, yes, and he is one of the finest puckhandling goaltenders ever and is just the second goaltender to score a goal in the playoffs (Ron Hextall being the first, with Philadelphia). Brodeur fulfilled his dream and scored into an empty net on April 17, 1997, against his hometown Canadiens.

In an era when goaltenders bulk up equipment and play a butterfly, flopping style, Brodeur is something of a throwback. His equipment is old

and small by comparison, and he plays a reflex, stand-up style. He is agile and athletic and as tough mentally as any goalie to stand in an NHL crease.

One of the few records left for Brodeur to break, which is owned by Roy, is combined regular-season and playoff wins. Roy has 702, but Brodeur sits just one behind. It's only a matter of time before another record falls and the legend of Brodeur grows.

Bet you didn't know

Martin Brodeur's father, Denis, is a noted hockey photographer, working for 20 years for the Montreal Canadiens. His collection of more than 115,000 photos are now in the possession of the NHL. Denis was also a pretty good goaltender in his day and earned an Olympic bronze medal with Canada in 1956, when the country was represented by the Kitchener-Waterloo Dutchmen in Italy.

Martin Brodeur, meanwhile, served as backup to Roy in the 1998 Olympics in Nagano, then helped Canada win its first gold medal in 50 years at the 2002 Games in Salt Lake City. He was also a member of the 2010 gold-medal-winning team in Vancouver.

The Brodeurs are the only father and son goaltenders to win medals in Olympic history.

Patrick Roy

There are legendary goalies who were simply great, and then there are legendary goalies who were great under pressure. Patrick Roy was both.

Little wonder "St. Patrick," as fans in Montreal came to call him, became the winningest goalie of all time, a record he eventually surrendered to Montreal native Martin Brodeur. Roy combined excellent goaltending skills with a fierce determination, making him one of the very few goalies to be feared whenever the stakes were the highest.

A native of Quebec City, Roy won four Stanley Cup championships with two different teams (two each with Montreal and Colorado) and won the Conn Smythe Trophy as playoff MVP in three of them. Although he didn't invent the butterfly style, one could argue he perfected it and, combined with a tremendous glove hand and a mental toughness even the best in the business would admire, he was a legend well before his career ended.

Roy exuded a confidence that bordered on cockiness, but he could back it up. A fiercely proud individual, he measured himself by his playoff performances. He would often say that the regular season was for money, the postseason was for pride. A pugnacious player, he seldom backed away from a fight and participated in two major brawls against Detroit while playing with archrival Colorado.

Inducted to the Hall of Fame in 2006, Roy is considered one of the greatest of all time.

Bet you didn't know

Roy's favourite goalie growing up in Quebec was Daniel Bouchard, who once gave a young Roy a goalie stick that Roy took to bed with him most every night. He also delivered one of the great put-down hockey quotes of all time when, responding to some trash talk from Chicago Blackhawks rival Jeremy Roenick, he said: "I can't hear what Jeremy is saying because I have two Stanley Cup rings plugging my ears."

In 1993, he set an NHL record with 10 overtime wins en route to winning the Stanley Cup. In addition to three Vezina Trophies, he won or shared the Jennings Trophy (fewest goals allowed) in 1987, 1988, 1989, 1992, and 2002. He led the league in shutouts and goals against average twice, was named a First Team All-Star four times, a Second Team All-Star twice, and played in 11 All-Star Games.

Dominik Hasek

In any debate regarding the best goalie in recent years, the names of Patrick Roy and Martin Brodeur head the list simply because they win. Yet Dominik Hasek, who started in relative obscurity in the Chicago Blackhawks system, is right there among the best.

Hasek, arguably the best of a stream of European imports, won two Stanley Cups in his NHL career (both with Detroit), but he is perhaps best known for his contributions to a usually offensively challenged Buffalo team. Hasek led the league in save percentage for five consecutive seasons with Buffalo (1995–99), something Brodeur has never done.

Hasek finished his NHL career with a .922 save percentage, Roy finished at .910 and Brodeur is currently at .914. According to the *New York Times*, Hasek's .922 career post-season save percentage is the second best since shot and save statistics were first recorded in newspapers in 1952. (Johnny Bower's .923 is the best.) Roy's was .918, and Brodeur's is .919.

Hasek has won six Vezina Trophies and is the only goalie to ever win back-to-back Hart Trophies as league MVP. He probably should have won three, having finished second to Eric Lindros in the lockout-shortened 1994–95 season when he became the first goalie in 20 years to finish with a goals-against average below 2.00.

He also led the Czech Republic to an Olympic gold medal in the 1998 Olympics in Nagano, beating Roy in a pivotal semi-finals game versus Canada while Brodeur was on the bench. His unorthodox style earned him the nickname "The Dominator." His style was "a flopper," but he was almost always in control of a style that both baffled and intimidated shooters.

Bet you didn't know

Hasek is well known for being the goaltender down and out when Brett Hull scored the controversial foot-in-the-crease goal that gave the Dallas Stars the 1999 Stanley Cup on perhaps the most controversial goal in the history of the NHL. A lesser known fact is that Hasek had his best year ever that season, posting a 1.77 goals-against average and a .939 save percentage.

Grant Fuhr

Durable (especially in the first 10 years of his career), acrobatic, mentally tough when the game was on the line—Grant Fuhr earned a reputation for being a winner playing with one of the great teams of all time, the Edmonton Oilers.

A native of Spruce Grove, Alberta, Fuhr joined what amounted to his hometown team just as the young Oilers were coming into their own. Edmonton was an NHL team on the verge of becoming a dynasty, and while the team in front of him was undeniably great, the players would acknowledge that Fuhr was a big part of their winning. He was in goal for four Stanley Cup wins with the Oilers over a 10-year span (they won a fifth while he was on the roster but suspended), and in 1987 played a stunning 4,304 minutes, winning 40 games.

Never a numbers player in the goals-against average or save-percentage columns, Fuhr simply won when the game was on the line. His lone Vezina Trophy came in 1987–88 when he also finished second to Mario Lemieux and ahead of teammate Wayne Gretzky in voting for the Hart Trophy. That year Fuhr led Team Canada to a win in the Canada Cup in what was arguably the greatest international hockey competition ever. He played all nine games and then appeared in 75 NHL regular-season games and 19 playoff games,

a testament to his physical and mental stamina. During the 1983–84 season, he recorded 14 points, the most ever for a goaltender in a single season. He also performed in the 1984 Canada Cup.

In later years, Fuhr moved through Toronto, Buffalo, Los Angeles, St. Louis, and Calgary with mixed results as a series of knee injuries started to take a toll. He did share a Jennings Trophy with Dominik Hasek in Buffalo at the end of the 1994 season and reunited briefly with Gretzky in Los Angeles. In a return to glory with the St. Louis Blues, Fuhr played in 79 games, starting 76 in a row, still an NHL record for the modern era.

He played in six All-Star games and was MVP of the 1986 contest. He was inducted into the Hockey Hall of Fame in 2003 in his first year of eligibility.

Bet you didn't know

Fuhr was in net when the Oilers set a record for the longest undefeated streak from the start of a season (15 games, 12-0-3). His most terrifying moment during his career may have come in the off-season when, never having learned to swim, he spent a summer rehabilitating a knee injury in a pool at the State University of New York at Buffalo. The water was always deep, but Fuhr used a flotation device to keep his head above water.

Ken Dryden

Critics would argue that Ken Dryden's greatness came from the great Montreal teams that played in front of him rather than from any single accomplishment on his part. Critics would be wrong.

Exceptionally tall amongst goaltenders at that time, Dryden ushered in the age of the supersized netminder and his style, even when down on the ice, was to take away as much of the net as possible. He did it in superb fashion, winning six Stanley Cups in eight seasons, all with the Canadiens. He also won the Conn Smythe Trophy as playoff MVP (1971), joining the Canadiens for the final two weeks of the season and leading them to upsets of the Boston Bruins and Chicago Black Hawks in the playoffs.

He then came back to win the Calder Trophy as rookie of the year the following season, an unheard of accomplishment both before and since. Dryden also won an NCAA championship while at Cornell University and was one of the goaltenders for Team Canada in the famed 1972 Summit Series. He once proved his value to legendary Canadiens general manager Sam Pollock by sitting out a season in a contract dispute while attending to his legal studies, a decision that likely cost the Canadiens any chance of winning the Cup in 1974.

Dryden had a short run as an NHLer, but it was by choice. In his brief time in the league he posted a .790 winning percentage, a 2.24 goals-against average, won 258 games (46 by shutout) while losing just 57 in a mere 397 NHL games. He won the Vezina Trophy five times and was also a five-time First Team All-Star.

Bet you didn't know

Because Ken Dryden jumped directly from college to the NHL, many think he was a Montreal draft pick. But Dryden was actually selected by the Boston Bruins in the 1964 Amateur Draft and traded to the Habs along with Alex Campbell for Paul Reid and Guy Allen. The Bruins are said to have initiated the deal as they coveted Allen, who played four seasons in the minors without ever seeing the NHL.

Bernie Parent

There was a time when the Philadelphia Flyers didn't have any problems in goal because they had Bernie Parent, a legend in the making, between the pipes. The native of Montreal started his career with Boston but joined the Flyers in the 1967 expansion draft. Parent wound up in Toronto, where he hooked up with his childhood idol Jacques Plante, who had a profound influence on his career.

Parent left for a season to play with Miami in the WHA. The team never got off the ground, but Parent ended up with the Philadelphia entry in the upstart league. A financial dispute led him back to the NHL after a season and he convinced the Leafs to move him back to the Flyers.

That's when he helped lead the Flyers to their first two (and to this day only) Stanley Cup championships, also winning the Conn Smythe and Vezina Trophy each time. Bobby Clarke might have been the heart of the Flyers in their expansion years, but Parent was by far their best player. Parent was durable (until an eye injury prematurely ended his career at age 34), blessed with a good glove hand, and perhaps the best "angle" goalie of all time. The popular refrain in Philadelphia in Parent's time was that: "only the Lord saves more than Bernie Parent."

His career was short and he was often overshadowed by the exploits of the "Broad Street Bullies," but Parent was one of the best of his time. He was elected to the Hockey Hall of Fame in 1984.

Bet you didn't know

Parent set the NHL record for games started (73) and games won 47, in 1973–74. The games-won mark was eventually surpassed by Martin Brodeur (48) in 2006–07, but Parent's 47 wins is still the NHL mark for games won in regulation time in a single season. During the 1970 playoffs, Parent tried to help Toronto teammate Jim Harrison, who was in a fight with the New York Rangers' Vic Hadfield. During the melee, Parent's mask was tossed into the Madison Square Garden crowd and not returned. Parent refused to play and was replaced by Jacques Plante. The mask was later returned.

Billy Smith

William John Smith always went by the name Billy, but he was also known as "Battlin' Billy," a goalie willing to fight on and off the ice. That was a good thing for a New York Islanders team that had to grow and learn how to win, a team that eventually turned into a dynasty, winning four Stanley Cups with Smith a key in net. In his own way, Smith often showed his teammates the way. Venture near his crease and an opponent was likely to remember that wicked slash across the ankles as often as that memorable save when the game was on the line.

Smith took no prisoners. There was only one way to play the game.

If you weren't giving your all and then some, you weren't giving enough, and Smith had no problem telling teammates as much. He was, in his time, the definition of a "money goalie."

Smith's style was dictated by one simple theory—whatever worked, be it poke check, glove save, butt end to an opponent's face, feigning injury to get a crucial timeout. If it helped the Islanders win, he did it. Smith was not about being popular; he wanted only to win. Like Grant Fuhr, he wasn't about statistical achievements, and he didn't win many NHL awards (though he does have one Vezina and Conn Smythe to his credit). He did, however, lead the NHL in postseason wins five times. For Smith, that's what it was all about: winning.

Bet you didn't know

It's well known that Smith refused to shake opponents' hands after a playoff series because he felt it was a "fake" congratulations, and he hated it. It's also well known that he is credited with the first goal scored by a goaltender in an NHL regular-season game even though it was actually shot into the net by Colorado Rockies defenceman Rob Ramage. Smith made a save, with the rebound going to Ramage who made a stray pass on a delayed penalty, his net empty, and that is where the puck wound up.

Tony Esposito

Tony Esposito, or "Tony O" as he quickly became known, won fame early in his goaltending career (rookie season, 1969–70) winning the Vezina and Calder Trophies and setting a league record for most shutouts in a single season (15). It was an accomplishment that positioned him to be runner-up for the Hart Trophy, a rarity for goaltenders of his era.

He was 26 at the time (considerably older than Tom Barrasso, who accomplished the same "double" at age 18), but he never looked back. In Esposito's time, the Black Hawks never failed to make the playoffs. Along the way he accumulated 76 shutouts playing his "butterfly" style.

He followed up his rookie season with his best shot ever at winning the Stanley Cup, a 1970–71 run in which the Hawks won the Western Division and advanced to the Stanley Cup Final. The team eventually lost in seven games to his original team, the Montreal Canadiens. The Hawks couldn't hold a third-period lead in that seventh game and wound up losing at home.

Esposito shared the Vezina the following season with teammate Gary Smith, compiling a stunningly low 1.77 goals-against average in the process. It was the second of three Vezina wins for Esposito, whose brother Phil was a prolific scorer with Chicago, Boston, and the New York Rangers.

Esposito had some international fame as well, sharing the goal with Ken Dryden during the 1972 Summit Series. He garnered Canada's first win in that series and finished with a better goals-against average than Dryden. He shared a third Vezina later in his career with Philadelphia's Bernie Parent. A fierce and admittedly nervous individual before games, he was a cool competitor on the ice. Esposito continued to play at a high level even when the Hawks started a long slide.

He was inducted into the Hockey Hall of Fame in 1988.

Bet you didn't know

Esposito was one of just eight goalies who won a Vezina while catching the puck with his right hand. He made his NHL debut (with the Montreal Canadiens) against Boston, forcing a 2-2 tie in a game in which his brother Phil scored both goals for the Bruins. The Canadiens let him go in the inter-league draft largely because they had Rogie Vachon and Gump Worsley in goal at the time. Though he represented Canada in the Summit Series and at the 1977 World Championships, he became a naturalized U.S. citizen and played for Team USA in the 1981 Canada Cup.

Gerry Cheevers

A money goaltender, Gerry Cheevers won a pair of Stanley Cups with great Bruins teams of the early 1970s. He was one of those goalies who would give up goals in a game but who could slam the door shut when it was needed most.

Cheevers played on Boston teams that were splendid offensively, with the likes of Bobby Orr and Phil Esposito guiding a gifted offence, but he was often left to fend for himself. Nevertheless, Cheevers found a way to get the job done. He had a 53-34 career playoff record, one of the finest percentages ever.

He was acrobatic and unorthodox at times, often rushing out at shooters to either surprise or cut the angles. He was also often criticized for his wandering style and his puckhandling, and he admitted to sometimes overhandling the puck, but more often than not he found a way to make the big save.

Cheevers played parts of seven seasons with the Bruins before departing for the WHA, where he starred with Cleveland Crusaders for four seasons, three times named an all-star and once named top goaltender. He returned to play for the Bruins for five more seasons and later coached Boston.

"Cheesie," as he was called, was inducted into the Hockey Hall of Fame in 1985.

Bet you didn't know

Gerry Cheevers created an iconic mask. He had the Bruins' trainer paint stitches on the mask each time he was struck by a puck. Not quite so well known is how that tradition started. By his own admission Cheevers was trying to get out of practice and had retired to the trainer's room after being hit on the mask by a shot that he later admitted, "wouldn't have cracked an egg." He didn't fool coach Harry Sinden, however, who ordered Cheevers back onto the ice. In order to "crack" the tension of the moment, Cheevers had the trainer paint the stitch marks on the mask to show what might have been had he been playing bare-faced, and the legendary mask was born.

Ed Belfour

Ed Belfour was never drafted by an NHL team but by the end of his stellar career he had 484 wins, the third best total in NHL history and likely his ticket to the Hockey Hall of Fame.

A fierce competitor, Belfour was dedicated to fitness. On the ice, he had a never-give-up-on-the-puck attitude, an exceptionally quick glove hand, and the agility to make his mark first with the Chicago Blackhawks, with which he landed in 1988, and later with the Dallas Stars. He also had stints with the San Jose Sharks, Toronto Maple Leafs, and Florida Panthers. He even played for a season in Europe at the end of his career.

Belfour compiled one of the best rookie seasons in NHL history, winning the Calder Trophy, the Vezina, and the Jennings, and he was a finalist for the Hart Trophy after a season in which he won 43 of 74 starts and posted a 2.47 goals-against average with the Blackhawks. He lost the Hart to Brett Hull of St. Louis, but he won the Vezina again in 1993,

and three more Jennings Trophies for fewest goals allowed.

Belfour, who led the Hawks to the Stanley Cup Final in 1992, had a brief stint with the Sharks but rebounded after he signed as a free agent with Dallas. In his first season with the Stars he had a 1.88 goals-against average and led Dallas to the President's Trophy and the Western Conference Final where the Stars were beaten by the Detroit Red Wings. The following season Belfour had a 1.99 GAA and led the Stars to a Stanley Cup championship, beating the Buffalo Sabres and star goaltender Dominik Hasek in a series highlighted by stellar goaltending at both ends of the ice.

Belfour made 53 saves to Hasek's 50 in the triple overtime final game won by the Stars, 2-1, on Brett Hull's controversial foot-in-the crease goal. In a remarkable display of mental and physical toughness, Belfour posted a 1.23 average in the final to Hasek's equally remarkable 1.68.

Bet you didn't know

Ed Belfour and Dominik Hasek were the first NHL goalies to be involved in a shootout when the league instituted the practice after the 2004–05 lockout. Belfour, playing for the Leafs at the time, lost on a shot by Ottawa's Dany Heatley.

Belfour picked up the nickname "Eddie the Eagle" because of paintings on his hockey mask. He played against the Florida Panthers in their first game, played with them in their 1,000th franchise game, and tied Terry Sawchuk's mark of 447 career wins while playing against them.

ORIGINAL SIX
DEFENCE

1. Doug Harvey
2. Eddie Shore
3. Leonard "Red" Kelly
4. Miles "Tim" Horton
5. Pierre Pilote
6. Harry Howell
7. Aubrey "Dit" Clapper
8. Emile "Butch" Bouchard
9. Bill Gadsby
10. Lionel Conacher

① Doug Harvey

What the great Bobby Orr was to his era, Doug Harvey was to his. And that is heady praise, indeed, for both men.

"As far as I'm concerned, he is far and away the best defenceman ever," legendary Montreal Canadiens coach "Toe" Blake once said.

That is debatable, of course. But there is no debating that Harvey was arguably the best defensive defenceman ever and in his own way was an innovator, a player who changed how defencemen played the game. "He changed the whole game," said teammate "Boom Boom" Geoffrion.

Harvey was great defensively, but he was also a terrific puckhandler who was supremely confident with dictating play. He could speed up a game with his puck-moving skills, or slow it down with his deft stickhandling. In many ways, he was also the first true offensive defenceman in the NHL. In an era when defencemen routinely chipped the puck out of their zone, Harvey would control the puck, welcome forecheckers to come after him, then make a nifty pass up the ice.

Many said he was the reason the great Canadiens teams of the 1950s were not only able to play "firewagon hockey" but first started playing that way. And when the Canadiens panicked and got into trouble in their own end, Harvey collected the puck and restored calm to proceedings by controlling the puck—a habit that led one sportswriter to call him "Dawdling Doug," a nickname that stuck.

"He was an early Bobby Orr, except he did it in semi-slow motion," said former NHL player and analyst Howie Meeker. "You always knew what was coming; you could see it happening, but you couldn't do anything about it."

Harvey, who was born in the west end of Montreal in 1924, was also the key to the Canadiens' great power play, which was so dangerous—often scoring twice or more on a single penalty—that in 1956 the NHL finally changed the rules, no longer making players serve the full two minutes, but instead ending the penalty when a power-play goal was scored.

Harvey was good at both ends of the rink, a great defender and an equally great playmaker. There wasn't a lot of flash and dash to his game—in fact, it was often said he could play in a rocking chair—but he could control a game. Harvey won the Norris Trophy, as the league's top defenceman, seven times from 1955 to 1962. The only season of those eight in which he didn't win, teammate Tom Johnson did. Only Orr, with eight Norris wins, has won the trophy more times than Harvey. He was also an All-Star for 11 straight years, a First Team All-Star in 10 of those years, and a Second Team selection the other.

In Harvey's 14 seasons with Montreal, playing on those powerhouse teams that included the likes of Jacques Plante, Jean Beliveau, Dickie Moore, "Rocket" Richard, Henri Richard, Johnson, and Geoffrion, Harvey won the Stanley Cup six times, including the record-setting five in a row during the late 1950s.

Harvey was named captain of the Canadiens in 1960 after "The Rocket" retired, but only held the title for one season before he was dealt to the New York Rangers, a move that baffled many, including Harvey. The Canadiens insisted it had to do with

↪ Doug Harvey takes his man out effectively along the boards.

his age and that it would allow him to be a player-coach, but Harvey believed it was punishment.

"It had to do with the union activities," Harvey said. "I was a First Team All-Star and won the Norris Trophy that year. You don't give away players like that."

In New York, he took over as player-coach and won that seventh Norris Trophy. He gave up the coaching portfolio after the first season and played two more with the Rangers, earning $30,000 as the highest-paid player in the league before he was left unprotected by the Rangers.

Harvey kicked around the minors for a few seasons, returned for a couple of games with the Detroit Red Wings, and finished his playing days with two more seasons with the expansion St. Louis Blues, joining them in the playoffs in their inaugural 1967–68 season. That spring and the next

he helped lead the Blues to the Stanley Cup Final, where they were twice swept by the Canadiens.

It was after that 1969 loss that Harvey retired for good from playing, coaching a year in junior and then working as an assistant coach with Houston of the WHA. Harvey finished his NHL career with 540 points in 1,113 games. Four times he had more than 40 points in a season and once had 50 points, big numbers for a defenceman at that time.

"He was the best defenceman of our day," said former Maple Leafs captain George Armstrong. "It's like playing against (Wayne) Gretzky and (Bobby) Orr. It didn't matter what they did, they always beat you."

Sadly, Harvey battled with alcoholism for many years, especially later in his life. In 1989, just days after celebrating his 65th birthday, Harvey died of cirrhosis of the liver.

○ Harvey checks Toronto's Frank Mahovlich as the "Big M" tries to move in on goalie "Gump" Worsley.

○ Stick in front for perfect technique, Harvey blocks the way of Toronto's Ted Hampson.

Bet you didn't know

Doug Harvey was inducted into the Hockey Hall of Fame in 1973, but he refused to attend the induction ceremony. Instead, Harvey reportedly went fishing.

According to the Hockey Hall of Fame archives, on July 5, 1973, Lefty Reid, who was the Hall's curator, sent a letter to Harvey congratulating him on his election to the Hall. On July 20, Reid received a letter of apology from Harvey's wife, Ursula, saying Doug had refused to accept his induction. Indeed, Harvey did not attend the ceremony. According to reports of the day, Harvey felt he should have been inducted a year earlier. He felt the league had passed judgment on his lifestyle. "Nothing but politics," said Harvey, "and that's one game I've never played. I plan to be out fishing."

That was not the first time Harvey marched to the beat of a different drummer. After he won his first Stanley Cup in 1953, when the Canadiens beat the Boston Bruins in the Final, Harvey refused to participate in the traditional handshake at the end of the series.

"I'm running them into the boards and banging them around one minute and because we win the Stanley Cup that's going to change?" Harvey said. "I don't really like them anyway. Why should I shake their hands?"

He was inducted into Canada's Sports Hall of Fame in 1975 and had his number 2 retired by the Habs on October, 26, 1985. In 1998, *The Hockey News* ranked Harvey sixth on the list of the 100 Greatest Players of all time.

Eddie Shore

If hockey had a Ty Cobb, it was defenceman Eddie Shore. Tough, skilled, demanding, uncompromising, and not above inflicting occasional pain, Shore played mostly for the Boston Bruins. He won four Hart Trophies as league MVP, the most of any defenceman and more than any forward not named Wayne Gretzky or Gordie Howe. He also won two Stanley Cups with the Bruins (in 1929 and '39) and became the model for the rugged "do-all" defenceman that shapes the game even to this day. His double digit goal-scoring exploits set the stage with the Bruins for the much later arrival of Bobby Orr.

Shore set an NHL record with 165 penalty minutes in his second season in the league, and he was so tough and mean that players were said to have put a bounty on his head (some of the contributors were allegedly his own teammates). He was once in a scuffle with teammates where he nearly lost an ear in a fierce battle during practice. Aside from his skills at controlling a hockey game like no other before him and few who followed, Shore is also known for nearly killing "Ace" Bailey when Bailey was with the Maple Leafs. Shore hit him from behind, fracturing Bailey's skull and ending his career. Shore received a 16-game suspension for that infraction but later made peace with Bailey and participated in a benefit game in his honour.

Bet you didn't know

At the end of his playing career, Shore purchased a minor league team, the Springfield Indians and quickly turned it into the place players didn't want to play. Shore was owner, manager, coach, trainer, and everything else necessary to run a team and not pay an employee to do some of the work. He once called a meeting of players' wives, asking them to withhold sex until the men played better. His actions led to a player revolt and he answered by selling the entire roster.

Leonard "Red" Kelly

Perhaps the prototype for the "can-do-it-all" player, Kelly was an outstanding defenceman who could—and later did—play forward. He was smart, skilled, and tough (in a gentlemanly way) and later became a coach. He played on more Stanley Cup winning teams (eight) than any player who never played for the Montreal Canadiens.

In 1954, Kelly was runner-up for the Hart Trophy and won the Norris Trophy as best defenceman, the first year it was awarded. He also won three Lady Byng trophies with Detroit and was a standout for both the Red Wings and the Toronto Maple Leafs. Kelly was the forerunner of a style of play that later made Bryan Trottier and Butch Goring famous. He could beat you offensively, defensively, with his smarts or his skill—and he won a lot.

In just over 12 seasons with the Red Wings, his team won eight regular-season championships and four Stanley Cups and he was a First Team All-Star defenceman six times. With the Leafs, Kelly played more often at forward, becoming the centre who set up Frank Mahovlich for the bulk of his goals. In eight seasons with the Leafs, he won another Byng and four more Stanley Cups, several of which came via his ability to shadow and slow if not completely shut down legendary Canadiens centre Jean Beliveau.

In 1,316 regular-season games, Kelly scored 281 goals and 542 assists for 823 points. At the time of his retirement, he was seventh all-time in career points, fifth in assists, thirteenth in goals, and second only to Gordie Howe in games played. In 164 playoff games, he scored 33 goals and 59 assists for 92 points.

⊍ Kelly is awarded the Bickell Cup.

Bet you didn't know

Kelly came to the Leafs because he refused a trade to the New York Rangers, telling the Red Wings he would retire if they made the deal. Leafs GM "Punch" Imlach intervened and brokered a deal for Kelly. When Kelly had played junior hockey, Leafs scouts told management he wouldn't last 20 games in the NHL. Most people know that, but there's more to the story. Kelly played much of his last season in Detroit with a fractured ankle. It was a secret, but Kelly let it slip after the season and Red Wings coach Jack Adams was furious, hence the trade. Kelly is famous as a Leafs coach, but he began his coaching career with the expansion Los Angeles Kings. Imlach even managed to put that job on hold until the Kings gave the Leafs a minor league player. Such was the fate of NHL players and retired players at that time.

4 Miles "Tim" Horton

Well before he was known for coffee and doughnuts, "Tim" Horton was known as a premier defenceman in the National Hockey League and, arguably, the strongest player to ever play the game. That's a boast not taken lightly. There were bigger and tougher defencemen before and after Toronto's legendary number 7, but Horton was so strong he could take a player into the corner and keep him there for as long as deemed necessary. Often it was with what amounted to a human bear hug—a ploy that's pretty much illegal for defencemen in today's game—but when Horton had a player in such a grip, the opponent ran the very serious risk of having his ribs crushed.

But there was more to Horton than strength. He had skill, smarts, and great skating ability and was one of the very first defencemen to master the then seldom-used slapshot. He used it to devastating effect, putting a low hard shot on net that, when it didn't beat the goalie outright, usually resulted in a rebound and scoring chance for a teammate.

Horton played 24 seasons in the NHL, mostly with the Leafs, but he also played in Pittsburgh, New York (Rangers), and Buffalo. In addition to his strength, he was known for his team-first attitude and hard work. He was a First Team All-Star three times and had the same number of Second Team honours. Horton never won a Norris Trophy, but then he played a different kind of game. He was a shutdown defenceman who could also rush the puck out of his own end, and he was a well-regarded shot blocker. In 1962 he set a Leafs record for points by a defenceman in the playoffs (16). It wasn't broken until 1994. He played from 1949 until 1974, the year of his death.

Bet you didn't know

Horton helped the Buffalo Sabres make the playoffs three years into their existence. The following year he died in a car crash driving from Toronto—where he had played and was a standout performer in the game—to Buffalo. He crashed his sports car, a De Tomaso Pantera, going more than 100 miles an hour down the Queen Elizabeth Way. He got the car from then GM "Punch" Imlach, who never quite got over Horton's death. "He told me it was a Ford [Ford distributed the car in the U.S. at the time]. I didn't want to, but he drove a tough bargain and I figured what the heck, it was a Ford, how much trouble could it be." Imlach had given Horton a pass from riding the team bus that night because the veteran player wanted to attend to some business matters with his fledgling chain of doughnut shops.

Pierre Pilote

Pilote went by the name of Pierre, but his middle name might well have been Norris. He was a three time recipient of the Norris Trophy as the league's best defenceman, winning in 1963, 1964, and 1965 and finishing second in voting in 1962, 1966, and 1967. Pilote, who grew up in Fort Erie, Ontario, and played minor hockey across the Niagara River in Buffalo with the AHL Bisons, was on the First or Second All-Star Team every year from 1960 to 1967. He not only was skilled, he was durable, playing 376 consecutive games at one point, an ironman streak of sorts in his time. He gained most of his fame playing with Elmer "Moose" Vasko for the Chicago Black Hawks. In their heyday, they were regarded as one of the all-time great blue-line tandems.

Pilote won a Stanley Cup with the Black Hawks in 1961 and the following year was named captain of the club that still had Bobby Hull and Stan Mikita on its roster. Pilote was a tough player, but he was also a skilled defenceman. Still, he once knocked out Henri and Maurice Richard during the same altercation in a game. He was a great shot blocker, but one who could also rush and pass the puck.

Pilote was inducted in the Hockey Hall of Fame in 1975.

Bet you didn't know

Like most Canadian-born hockey players, Pilote learned to skate at a young age, but he didn't play organized hockey between the ages of 14 and 17 because a fire had destroyed the local rink. In a rare display of organizational good judgment, the Black Hawks retired the number 3 worn by Pilote and Keith Magnuson in a co-ceremony at United Center in 2008. "Pete" is one of a handful of players whom Canada Post honoured with his own postage stamp, in 2005. When he got the call from Buffalo to go to the NHL, he called his parents and told them his first NHL game would be against the Maple Leafs in Toronto. They lived about 100 miles from the Gardens but he told them not to bother to come because "they probably won't play me."

Harry Howell

There are great players who streak through the NHL like a comet, and then there's Harry Howell. Consistent, durable, loyal, and talented, Howell gained fame as a solid stay-at-home defenceman with the New York Rangers. He played 1,411 NHL games, an astounding 1,160 with the Rangers, where he represented the team in seven All-Star Games starting in 1954 and extending to 1970. Cool, calm, smart, a smooth skater, and always with the ability to make the right play at the right time, Howell was embraced by the notorious Rangers fans as what a Ranger player should be, a player who performed well and bled Rangers blue.

Howell played 17 seasons with the Rangers and another five in the NHL with the Oakland/California Golden Seals and the Los Angeles Kings and three more in the World Hockey Association with New York/New Jersey, San Diego, and Calgary. When he left the NHL he did so having played more games on the blue line than any other NHL player and remains sixth all-time in games played at defence. Howell also coached in the NHL (with Minnesota) and later was a longtime scout for a number of teams. In his best year, Howell made First Team All Star (1966–67) and won the Norris Trophy. He was inducted into the Hockey Hall of Fame in 1979.

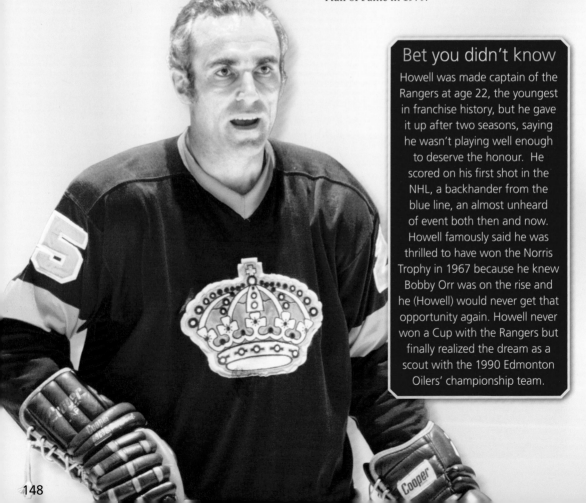

Bet you didn't know

Howell was made captain of the Rangers at age 22, the youngest in franchise history, but he gave it up after two seasons, saying he wasn't playing well enough to deserve the honour. He scored on his first shot in the NHL, a backhander from the blue line, an almost unheard of event both then and now. Howell famously said he was thrilled to have won the Norris Trophy in 1967 because he knew Bobby Orr was on the rise and he (Howell) would never get that opportunity again. Howell never won a Cup with the Rangers but finally realized the dream as a scout with the 1990 Edmonton Oilers' championship team.

Aubrey "Dit" Clapper

When people speak of "old-time hockey," even in the movie *Slap Shot*, one of the players they always mention is Dit Clapper. It's understandable. Playing with the Boston Bruins, Clapper became the first skater in NHL history to play 20 seasons. He also coached the Bruins for two seasons as a player-coach and for two more seasons after ending his playing days. Clapper played more than a bit of forward for the Bruins and scored an important goal from his right wing position when the Bruins won the franchise's first Stanley Cup, in 1929. He scored 41 goals in 44 games the following season, but despite that success he was moved back to defence the following season where he gained even more fame.

He teamed with another old-time hockey legend, Eddie Shore, and keyed another Stanley Cup win for the Bruins in 1939. Between that season and 1941 Clapper was named an NHL First Team All-Star three times. The Bruins retired his famed number 5 sweater in 1947 after he had scored 228 goals and 474 points in the regular season and 13 goals in the playoffs. That same year he was inducted into the Hockey Hall of Fame when the Hall waived the regular waiting period as a tribute to his exceptional talents.

Bet you didn't know

Clapper was big for his era (6'2", 200 lbs.) and had his share of physical confrontations, but he was considered too talented to be just a fighter. That said, he did punch Clarence Campbell, later to be NHL President, in the mouth. It was during a game when Campbell was a referee and missed a call. Clapper was fined $100 but not suspended, in part because Campbell admitted he swore at Clapper while escorting him to the penalty box.

⑧ Emile "Butch" Bouchard

Behind and alongside a great rushing defenceman there is usually an equally great stay-at-home defenceman. "Butch" Bouchard was just that for legendary Montreal Canadiens defenceman Doug Harvey.

Bouchard was big, strong, extremely physical, and usually the last line of defence whenever Harvey went up ice. Playing with the Habs from 1941 to 1956, Bouchard won four Stanley Cups with the club, was captain for eight seasons, and made the All-Star Team four times. His strength, aside from his exceptional physical strength, was his ability to make good first-strike passes that sent Harvey and the forwards clear of their zone, and his ability to defend whenever Harvey or anyone else was caught up ice.

Bouchard had exceptional defensive and passing skills. He also was good at reading plays and breaking them up before they became problematic. It was as much an art as a science and coupled with a superior work ethic served him well as the Canadiens rebounded from a string of mediocre seasons to prominence and four Stanley Cups with Bouchard in the lineup. He was a First Team All-Star three times in succession (1945, 1946, and 1947) and was a Second Team selection in 1944. He was inducted into the Hockey Hall of Fame in 1996 and is one of only a handful of hockey players to have received the Order of Canada.

Bet you didn't know

The Quebec Major Junior Hockey League Defenceman of the Year Award is named in Bouchard's honour. On the 100th anniversary of the Canadiens' birth, Bouchard's famed number 3 (along with Elmer Latch's number 16) became the 16th (and 17th) retired numbers. Bouchard's final game came on April 10, 1956, and most of it passed on the bench partly because of his age and partly because he had been slowed by knee injuries. Coach "Toe" Blake sent him out in the final minute to a rousing ovation, and it was he who was called forward to accept the Stanley Cup as the Canadiens defeated the Detroit Red Wings in the last game of the final season of Bouchard's career.

Bill Gadsby

Bill Gadsby played 20 years in the NHL and never won a Stanley Cup, but by every other measure he was a champion.

After just 12 games in the minors he was called up by the Chicago Black Hawks and never looked back, establishing himself as a fixture on the blue line for the Black Hawks, the New York Rangers, and the Detroit Red Wings. He had early success as a Black Hawks forward, but he came into his own with the Red Wings and nearly won a Cup, losing the final game of a six-game series to the Montreal Canadiens in 1966.

Gadsby, who had a strong all-around game, was a First Team All-Star three times and a Second Team All-Star four times. He played 1,248 regular season games but mostly with poor teams, and he saw action in only 67 playoff games. He was best known for his defensive game, but in the 1958–59 season he set an NHL record for assists by a defenceman with 46, a surprisingly high number given it was a time when defensive hockey reigned supreme. He had a brief role as head coach with the Red Wings (one season) and was elected to the Hall of Fame in 1970.

Bet you didn't know

Gadsby made it to the Cup final three times in his career, but the closest he got to a win was the last time, in 1966. He was said to have endured some 600 stitches to his face during his career, but he also had an insurance policy that paid him $5 a stitch, making the number somewhat suspect. That said, Gadsby had a reputation for fearlessness and often put himself in front of shots. He felt blocking shots was every bit as important as making them.

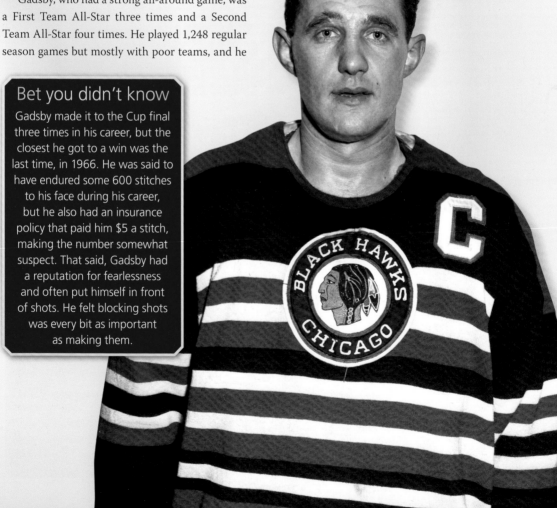

Lionel Conacher

Nicknamed "The Big Train," Conacher gained fame first as an exceptional all-around athlete and later as a hockey player. He excelled at Canadian and U.S. football, rugby, baseball, boxing, wrestling, and lacrosse, but he gained fame as an NHL defenceman from 1925 to 1937 during a time that pre-dated the Original Six. Conacher played with the Pittsburgh Pirates, New York Americans, Chicago Black Hawks, and Montreal Maroons, winning Cups with the Hawks and the Maroons.

Ironically, in the early days of his broad athletic career, hockey was Conacher's weakest sport. He did not start skating until he was 16 years old but because of his athletic ability he quickly closed the talent gap and in his best season finished second to Montreal's Aurele Joliat in voting for the Hart Trophy. Conacher became one of the better skaters in the NHL, but the strength of his game was physical play in his own zone, exceptional leadership skills, and a win-at-all-costs mentality that he carried over from his other sporting endeavours.

Bet you didn't know

Conacher played in the first hockey game ever broadcast on radio, a match involving his North Toronto Seniors and Midland, February 8, 1923. In 1921, he hit a game-winning home run for his Toronto-based baseball team, giving it a semi-pro championship, and then took a taxi across town to join his lacrosse team to score four goals. He joined the game in progress and with his team down by three.

He also scored a pair of touchdowns to give the Toronto Argos a Grey Cup win in 1921. Conacher served in the Ontario Legislature and as a member of parliament. A charter member of Canada's Sports Hall of Fame in 1955, the Canadian Football Hall of Fame and Museum in 1963, and the Canadian Lacrosse Hall of Fame and Museum in 1966, he was elected to the Hockey Hall of Fame in 1994, 40 years after his untimely death.

MODERN ERA
DEFENCE

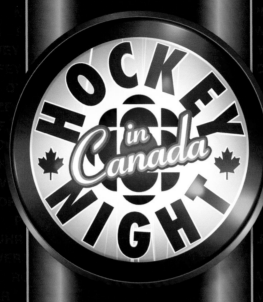

1. **BOBBY ORR**
2. **NICKLAS LIDSTROM**
3. **RAY BOURQUE**
4. **DENIS POTVIN**
5. **LARRY ROBINSON**
6. **PAUL COFFEY**
7. **SCOTT NIEDERMAYER**
8. **SCOTT STEVENS**
9. **BRAD PARK**
10. **AL MACINNIS**

① Bobby Orr

He is arguably the greatest player—and not just the greatest defenceman—to ever play the game: Number 4, Bobby Orr. The native of Parry Sound, Ontario, revolutionized the game, forever changing the way defencemen played and eventually how the position was defined. Orr made defence a position that had an impact at both ends of the rink.

"What can I say? Bobby was the greatest player who ever lived or ever will live," said his former Boston Bruins coach, Don Cherry. "Bobby Clarke said it best one time when he said it's a shame there's not a higher league he could have gone to."

Indeed, also a shame is that injuries prevented the incomparable Orr from dominating the NHL for more years than he did. Orr was a master at controlling play in his own end and his opponent's. He was a tremendous skater, powerful and sturdy on his blades. He at times looked like he was accelerating even when he was gliding on the ice.

Orr could take the puck in his end, rush it up the ice, and do laps with it in the opposition's zone if necessary. A superb puckhandler, he would either make the perfect pass or score himself. He could control and dominate a game with his skating and puckhandling skills.

As great as he was offensively, though, Orr was just as good defensively. He would block shots, win battles in front of the net, throw body checks. He wasn't afraid to drop the gloves when need be. He won the Norris Trophy eight consecutive years, the Hart Trophy three times, the Conn Smythe Trophy twice and, incredibly, led the league in scoring in the regular season twice, something no other defenceman has done before or since.

Orr helped lead the Bruins to two Stanley Cup victories, including their first in 29 years in 1970, one that is forever remembered for Orr scoring the final goal in overtime and flying through the air, tripped as he beat St. Louis Blues goaltender Glenn Hall. That spring he had 20 points in 14 playoff games.

"That was my greatest day in hockey," Orr said. "Life as a professional player is pretty darn good, but that was a great event." He led the Bruins to that second Stanley Cup win in 1972, this time producing 24 points in 15 post-season games.

Along the way, he became the first defenceman to score more than 40 goals in a season and the first player to earn more than 100 assists in a season. He had 46 goals in 1974–75 and 102 assists in 1970–71. And, during that 1969–70 season, he became the first 100-point defenceman in NHL history.

Orr, whose rights were owned by Boston when he was 14, played junior with the Oshawa Generals and joined the Bruins when he was 18. He earned a point in his first game, against Detroit, and went on to win the Calder Trophy and be named to the Second All-Star Team. But that season Orr also hurt his left knee while rushing with the puck, an injury that would trouble him throughout his career and ultimately cut it horribly short.

Orr had had six operations on that left knee by 1976. He was unable to play for Team Canada in the historic Summit Series with the Soviets in 1972, although he did travel and practice with the team. Fortunately, despite the knee miseries, Orr was able to play in the 1976 Canada Cup, leading Team Canada, maybe the best team ever, to victory.

Orr had a messy departure from the Bruins in 1976. He had played just 10 games in the 1975–76 season and believed the Bruins weren't keen on keeping him around, although there were allegations that his agent, Alan Eagleson, didn't

keep Orr fully informed of what was transpiring in contract negotiations.

Regardless, Orr wound up signing with the Chicago Black Hawks, playing 20 games the first season, missing a year after recovering from a sixth knee operation, then playing just six games before, sadly, the knee woes forced him to retire in November 1978 at the age of 30.

A man of great integrity, Orr refused to be paid by the Black Hawks because he didn't play. He remained with the club as an assistant coach after retiring, then became a player agent.

Orr's best season statistically was 1970–71 when he finished with 139 points and was plus-124. He had a 135-point season four years after that and strung together six consecutive 100-point plus seasons and was the league's plus-minus leader six times. Over his dozen dominant and brilliant years in the NHL, Orr played just 657 games, but finished with 270 goals and 915 points. He had another 92 points in 74 playoff games.

As great as Orr was—the best defenceman ever—hockey people often wondered how much greater he could have been had he played on two healthy knees. At the very least, he could have played much longer. Orr was inducted into the Hockey Hall of Fame in 1979.

◑ This iconic image shows Orr diving to knock a puck away, off balance but never giving up.

Orr moves in on the Toronto goal, an image of a defenceman in such
an offensive position rare before number 4 got to the NHL.

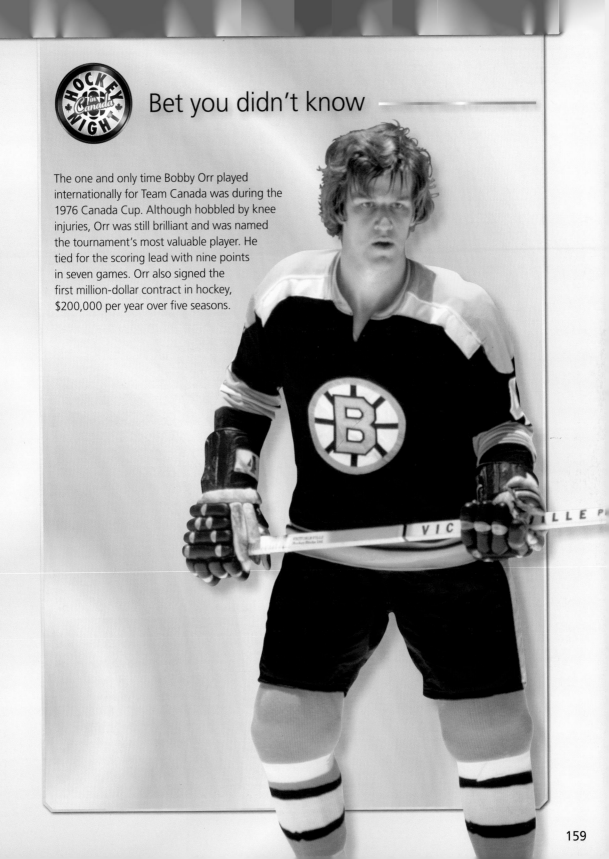

Bet you didn't know

The one and only time Bobby Orr played internationally for Team Canada was during the 1976 Canada Cup. Although hobbled by knee injuries, Orr was still brilliant and was named the tournament's most valuable player. He tied for the scoring lead with nine points in seven games. Orr also signed the first million-dollar contract in hockey, $200,000 per year over five seasons.

Nicklas Lidstrom

When Nicklas Lidstrom set sail for North America in 1991, few would have guessed he'd stay two decades and become the most decorated European NHL player of all time. He has won four Stanley Cups, six Norris Trophies, a Conn Smythe Trophy, and is still going

strong. His 1,000 points ranks among the top 10 active NHL points leaders.

It's safe to say that if a few teams could go back to the 1989 draft, they would not let him fall to 53rd overall. But he wasn't even Detroit's first pick that year, just another solid prospect from the little known Vasteras club team, with 23 points in 38 games his final season in Sweden.

Lidstrom arrived in the NHL just as Swedish pioneers such as Borje Salming were wrapping up their careers, but Lidstrom, along with Mats Sundin, Daniel Alfredsson, and Markus Naslund, would take that assimilation a step further by being named captains of their respective teams.

When Lidstrom accepted the Cup from commissioner Gary Bettman in 2008, he did so as the league's first European-trained captain. There had been little doubt as to who should inherit Steve Yzerman's 'C' when the latter retired in 2006. Lidstrom rarely took a night off or even a shift, missing less than 10 games a year.

Lidstrom has been incredibly resilient, playing two full 84-game regular seasons, his longest absence in any year eight games. He fell below 25 minutes of ice time per night only in the past couple of seasons. He has represented his country four times during the Olympics, winning gold in 2006 and captaining the team in 2010.

Bet you didn't know

Lidstrom turned into one of the NHL's greatest post-season performers with 175 points in 247 games, all with Detroit. On April 23, 2010, he passed Mark Messier in career playoff games with 237 and trails only Chris Chelios (266) and Patrick Roy (247).

Ray Bourque

Rarely will the ardent pro-sports fans of Boston cheer hard for a rival athlete to win a championship when he doesn't play on one of their beloved teams, never mind if he was born outside Massachusetts.

But when Ray Bourque won his first Stanley Cup as a member of the Colorado Avalanche in 2001, the cheers could be heard all the way from Boston Common. Bourque was like a son to Boston and a father figure to Bruins' players, earning their respect and admiration as the leader of the Bruins through the 1980s and '90s, during which time he won five Norris Trophies and was runner-up on five other occasions.

In lean years, the captain's outstanding offensive forays often provided the team's only highlights, but the Bruins missed the playoffs in only two years of his tenure. Chosen eighth overall in the famous 1979 draft class (all 21 selections made the NHL) Bourque sits fourth in NHL career assists with 1,169 and eighth in games played with 1,612. In the course of three decades in the game, he was a First Team All-Star 13 times, commencing in 1980 and ending in 2001.

Obtained with a pick that originally belonged to Los Angeles, Bourque scored in his first game, against the Winnipeg Jets, and was selected Calder Trophy winner as rookie of the year for 1979–80 (Wayne Gretzky was ineligible).

Bet you didn't know

The Bourque name is still hot on two NHL fronts. Ray's eldest son Chris is a left winger who had four points in 21 games for the Washington Capitals in 2009–10 and later that year was AHL playoff MVP. Ryan Bourque, drafted by the New York Rangers in 2009, won a gold medal with the Team USA juniors at the 2010 U20 World Championships.

Denis Potvin

When you hear the boards creak in the old Nassau County Coliseum these days, it can probably be traced to Denis Potvin loosening the bolts with 15 years of big hits and thousands of shots and clearing bank passes. Potvin wasn't just a fluid defenceman with three Norris Trophies to his credit; he racked up more than 1,600 penalty minutes, far more than other all-star defencemen of the day. He often fought some of the heavyweights in the NHL's "slap shot era."

But Potvin is most remembered for helping take the New York Islanders from doormats to dynasty. When he retired in 1988, the Isles had won the Cup four times and been to the final a fifth, while his 1,052 points stood for many years as a record for defencemen.

Tagged for greatness when he emerged from the Ottawa 67's (123 points in 1972–73), Potvin put in some long nights with the expansion Isles before the club started to see improvements through other high draft picks. Potvin became captain in 1979, just as the Isles set about to win four straight Cups (1980–83), the first true powerhouse of the NHL's post-expansion age.

Potvin would never change his Island address and contributed a 50-point season the year he departed. Following old boss Bill Torrey to Florida, the media savvy Potvin became a Panthers' colour analyst for many years.

Bet you didn't know

Potvin's hit on Ulf Nilsson of the Rangers, the one that broke the forward's ankle and still prompts a derogatory personal chant on game night at Madison Square Garden, was judged by most of those present to be a fairly clean hit and fluke injury. "It's just one of those things that are passed from one generation to the next," Potvin said of his hearing his name cursed for the hit so many years later. "Kind of like season tickets."

Larry Robinson

The Montreal Canadiens' outstanding defensive record in the 1970s, when they won six Stanley Cups, was not all about goaltending. It can also be traced to shutdown soldiers such as Larry Robinson, whose arrival as a regular on the Habs' blue line coincided with four seasons of under 200 goals against and five more at 240 or less.

Tall yet mobile, he was part of the strong core that included Guy Lapointe and Serge Savard, but Robinson won two Norris Trophies outright and was a First or Second Team All-Star in three of Montreal's four straight title years. With the plus-minus stat coming into vogue around the time of his arrival in the league, Robinson was calculated at a remarkable plus-730 in his long career.

The Eastern Ontario farm boy, nicknamed "Big Bird," came to prominence in the mid '70s when the Canadiens had to show they could out-hit and out-fight the reigning champion Philadelphia Flyers, as well as out-skate and out-score them. When the '76 Final opened, Robinson scored a big goal in

Game 1 and leveled the Flyers' Gary Dornhoefer with a huge body check in Game 2. "They had to bring hammers and crowbars to fix the dent in the boards," recalled Montreal netminder Ken Dryden. "It was a symoblic moment."

Robinson spent 17 years in Montreal and three more with the Los Angeles Kings. His teams never failed to make the playoffs and he appeared in more than 1,600 games. Robinson also won a Cup as coach of the New Jersey Devils in 2000, having taken the job late in the season and staying on to nearly get another ring before losing a Game 7 to Colorado.

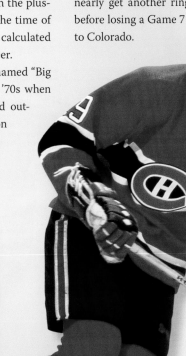

Bet you didn't know

Robinson was good, but the talent and seniority system on the Canadiens was so strong that he was kept in the minors in Nova Scotia for a year and a half when other struggling teams might have sent him out as soon as he graduated from the Kitchener Rangers. His first game wasn't until January 8, 1973, and he wasn't used in the first round of Montreal's playoff series against Buffalo. But he got his chance and his name is on the 1973 Cup, the first of nine times as player, coach, and scout.

Paul Coffey

Many hockey purists claim the position Paul Coffey played through most of his 21 NHL seasons didn't really exist. It wasn't defence, as he took off on a whim to join the rush and make some plays as dazzling as Oilers' teammates Wayne Gretzky and Jari Kurri. Yet it wasn't forward, either, as no winger could get back and help out as quickly as Coffey did in two or three effortless strides. Many called him a re-born rover from the days when seven men per team flooded the ice in the early 1900s.

But there was no question he could fly, both on the young, free-wheeling Oilers and later with eight other teams in a 1,400-game Hall of Fame career. He was the first draft pick the expansion Oilers were granted after a year in the league and by his second season, he was closing in on 100 points and was a Second Team All-Star. He would win three Norris Trophies and have his name on the Oilers' first three Stanley Cup wins, but he also became one of the first to leave in a contract dispute with general manager Glen Sather, an issue that foreshadowed the end of the small-market dynasty.

He won another Cup with Pittsburgh, sharing it with boyhood Toronto pal Larry Murphy, another high-scoring defender. Coffey's blazing speed did not desert him for another decade, through three Canada Cup wins. During the so-called "dead puck era" when he was inducted into the Hockey Hall of Fame, Coffey lamented, "a lot of teams don't allow players to make the plays now," a situation remedied after the lockout. He was a 100-point defenceman five times.

Bet you didn't know

Coffey wasn't a keen student of skating dynamics until he reached the NHL. "When I was younger, I was intrigued by skates, blades, and glides, but it was Barrie Stafford, our Oilers' trainer, who asked me if I'd ever considered changing the hull of my boot," Coffey recalled. "He was very helpful to me early on." Coffey's best year was 138 points for Edmonton in 1985–86, one behind Bobby Orr's record.

Scott Niedermayer

If the Hockey Hall of Fame ever wanted to open an annex in Western Canada, it could just ask Scott Niedermayer's permission to let fans come through his living room. Visitors could look at his impressive list of souvenirs from winning every major North American and international championship: the Memorial Cup, World Junior Championship, senior World Championship gold, two Olympic gold medals, four Stanley Cups, and the World Cup. Oh, and check out his Norris Trophy and Conn Smythe Trophy on the way out.

Offensive talent was clearly on his side as his 100-point season for the Cranbrook, B.C. midget team showed, but so was timing. He joined the Kamloops Blazers of the early 1990s, one of the best Canadian junior teams of the day and in '92 was Memorial Cup MVP with 23 points.

Drafted by the New Jersey Devils with the third overall pick they'd acquired from Toronto, Niedermayer joined a burgeoning club on its way to three Cups in the next 12 years. Some didn't appreciate the conservative tactics of the Devils, but Niedermayer routinely scored in double figures and achieved between 30 and 40 assists annually.

His leadership qualities made him an integral part of the 2002 Canadian Olympic team that ended a half-century drought without gold, and eight years later he captained the same club that won the title in his home province of British Columbia at the 2010 Olympics.

His fourth Cup came as a member of the Anaheim Ducks with brother Rob in 2007 and after changing his mind a couple of times about retirement, he announced in June 2010 that he was through, with 740 points in almost 1,300 games and 202 playoff appearances.

Bet you didn't know

An avid environmentalist and animal rights crusader, Scott Niedermayer sent a letter to Chicago City Council in 2007, urging them to uphold a ban on allowing local restaurants to put foie gras on the menu. "As an Anaheim Duck, I hate to see real ducks tortured so that a handful of wealthy chefs can serve their diseased organs," Niedermayer wrote to the politicians. He also championed a hydrogen-powered, zero-emission car.

Scott Stevens

He made no apologies for hitting opponents like a truck, believing those who didn't keep their heads up as he met them in the intersection were putting themselves at risk.

"It's a hockey game; it's not figure skating," Stevens said to any critics who thought he wanted to deliberately injure opponents with his broadside body checks. "I don't get a free ride, and no one gets a free ride from me."

He did leave a trail of groggy players in his wake and many suffered concussions. But Stevens was much more than a physical presence, compiling 908 points in 1,635 games. Twice runner-up for the Norris Trophy, he settled for five All-Star Team nominations and all three Stanley Cups won by New Jersey.

Inducted to the Hall of Fame in his first year of eligibility in 2007 (ironically, a slap shot that struck his head caused career-ending post-concussion syndrome), he turned to coaching with the Devils.

Born in Kitchener, Ontario, Stevens grew up a Maple Leafs fan and in another career quirk, had been a huge fan of Toronto defenceman Borje Salming, who rarely relied on punishing open-ice hits. Stevens was drafted fifth overall by Washington in 1982 and was promoted quickly as a teenager, proving so durable that he reached 1,500 games played faster than any NHLer.

After a 65-point season in 1984–85, the Caps considered shifting Stevens to the wing, but he was an anchor on defence right until the 2003–04 season when he retired a plus-393 with several regular season and playoff longevity records for his position.

Bet you didn't know

The Stevens brothers—Scott, Geoff, and Mike—used to play boisterous hockey games inside the family home and hacked up valuable family furniture in the process. "There was actually one room that Mom refused to decorate until we were (moved) out of the house," Scott said during his 2007 Hall of Fame induction. "I think that's how I got so competitive. With two brothers close to your age, you learn to hold your own."

Brad Park

The perception is that Brad Park had to settle for playing in Bobby Orr's shadow. While it is true that he was runner-up for the Norris trophy six times in his career (four to Orr, twice to Denis Potvin), the very talented offensive defenceman would make his own mark as the 1970s went on.

Park was a graduate of the Toronto Marlboros system when it routinely churned out stars, winning the 1967 Memorial Cup. And though ignored by his hometown Maple Leafs at draft time, he was welcomed to a Rangers' organization that had been out of the playoffs in a six-team league much of the 1940s, '50s, and '60s.

Coached by the great Fred Shero in the minors with Buffalo, Park eventually graduated to the parent team as it was turning the corner, making the 1972 Cup final against Boston. Park, who studied Orr on film and never voiced resentment about how the two players were judged, would play five years longer than Orr, in a larger media market, and would eventually fill some of the injured Orr's role when traded to the Boston Bruins in a mid-'70s mega-deal.

When Orr was hurt, Park played against the Soviets in the historic '72 Summit Series and finished strong with Team Canada, winning the eight-game series. And Park, not Orr, was given the chance to coach in the NHL, albeit briefly in the 1980s.

Park was named to the Hall of Fame in 1988, based on 17 seasons and 896 points.

Bet you didn't know

The Rangers and Bruins ended the 1960s as two of the worst playoff outfits in the six-team league. Yet in the 17 years Park was healthy and in New York or Boston, those clubs never missed post-season action. Park had 20 post-season points in 1977–78 with the Bruins and 125 in 161 games overall. But he never won the Stanley Cup.

Al MacInnis

He fired the shot heard 'round the hockey world. When Al MacInnis wound up, goaltenders' winced, defencemen prayed, and his own teammates got the heck out of the way.

From peppering hundreds of pucks at an old carpet hung along the side of his family barn (his father worked at an arena where extra pucks were plentiful), MacInnis developed the release that paid off in 379 regular season and playoff goals.

"Every other Canadian kid wanted to play in the NHL, but I was just (practice shooting) for a pastime," MacInnis recalled upon his election to the Hockey Hall of Fame in 2007. "I think that's where the saying, 'you couldn't hit the broadside of the barn' comes from. I never hit a cow or any of the other animals, though. My town (Port Hood, Nova Scotia) is a small fishing village of 900 and if it wasn't a beach day, there wasn't anything to do (but work on his shot). Never did I think I would ever play in the NHL. It was another planet away."

MacInnis moved to Kitchener, Ontario, where he eventually partnered with fellow Hall of Famer Scott Stevens on the OHL Rangers' blue line en route to a Memorial Cup. In addition to his shooting eye, MacInnis had more than 1,000 assists, residuals from getting hard-to-handle shots on or near the goal. Seven times he won the NHL All-Star Game skills' hardest-shot contest, but his greatest accomplishments were the 1989 Stanley Cup with the Calgary Flames and with it the Conn Smythe Trophy.

Bet you didn't know

MacInnis was in his prime when one-piece composite hockey sticks became popular in the NHL, but he stuck with wood throughout his 21 years in the league. When not practising his lethal shot, he would try and perfect slap passes and outlet passes that took advantage of opponents and goalies bracing for a direct shot and opening up other scoring options.

ALL-TIME

COACH

1. WILLIAM "SCOTTY" BOWMAN
2. AL ARBOUR
3. HECTOR "TOE" BLAKE
4. DICK IRVIN
5. GLEN SATHER
6. FRED SHERO
7. GEORGE "PUNCH" IMLACH
8. JACK ADAMS
9. TOMMY IVAN
10. ROGER NEILSON

William "Scotty" Bowman

He is the winningest coach in NHL history—most games won, most Stanley Cups won. You would expect the two would go together.

And the championships just keep on coming, though Bowman is no longer behind the bench. He finished his distinguished coaching career in the spring of 2002 with the Red Wings, appropriately winning his final game as Detroit captured the Stanley Cup for the third time under his guidance.

That night, after the Red Wings had dispatched the Carolina Hurricanes in five games, Bowman did something no other NHL coach has done. He put on a pair of skates and took the Stanley Cup for a spin around Joe Louis Arena. Bowman had won the Cup twice with the Red Wings and twice with the Pittsburgh Penguins, but only one of those wins came as a coach. Prior to that, Bowman won the Stanley Cup five times with the Montreal Canadiens, coaching some of the greatest teams ever assembled.

In the spring of 2010, Bowman added a 12th championship ring to his collection (nine as a coach, three as an executive) and while all were special, this one had an extra emotional attachment. Bowman won it together with his son, Stan, after the Chicago Blackhawks defeated the Philadelphia Flyers in six games. The elder Bowman served as a senior advisor to the Blackhawks, and Stan was the general manager.

It was almost as though the Bowmans had come full circle as a family. It was in 1973, soon after Bowman won his first Stanley Cup with the Canadiens, beating Chicago in that Final, that his wife Suella gave birth. That June, a boy named after the Stanley Cup arrived in the world.

"I just said, 'if we have a boy, let's name him Stanley'," recalled Scotty of the conversation he had with his wife in 1973. "Stanley Glenn. Glenn was after Glenn Hall. My first three years in the league, as a young coach, he was a big reason we were where we were."

The veteran Hall, who starred for years himself with the Blackhawks, was Bowman's goaltender with the St. Louis Blues in the first three seasons of expansion. All three years the Blues went to the Final, all three years they lost, never winning a game. But that wasn't about coaching; it was about the disparity between the Original Six and the expansion teams. Indeed, the hockey world took notice of a young coach named "Scotty" Bowman.

"I'm very pleased for Stan," said the elder Bowman after the Hawks won their first Cup since 1961. "He's had to deal with a lot off the ice. It's been tough with his health. I wanted him to get his name on the Cup. Stan presented me with the Cup and that was a special moment."

And the Bowman tradition continues.

"Scotty" Bowman only left the Red Wings to join the Chicago organization because of the chance to work with and spend time with Stan, who endured a battle with cancer in 2008, when he was assistant GM.

Bowman had worked in the Canadiens' minor-league system after his own playing career ended in junior hockey following a head injury. He was brought back to the Montreal organization by legendary general manager Sam Pollock after those few seasons in St. Louis, and named coach of the Habs in 1971.

He won that first Stanley Cup in his second season behind the bench and captured four straight from 1976 to 1979, coaching arguably

the greatest team ever in 1976–77, the Canadiens finishing with a gaudy 60-8-12 record, their 132 points a league record. Later, Bowman won a record 62 games with Detroit.

But after that fifth Cup win, when it was apparent Bowman would not be replacing Pollock as GM, he decided to leave the pressure cooker in Montreal with five Cup wins in eight seasons to his credit. He went to Buffalo as coach and general manager, although he was unable to build a winner with the Sabres.

Bowman was hired by the Penguins as director of player personnel and won yet another Stanley Cup in 1991. The following season he returned to the bench with the Penguins after the tragic death of Bob Johnson and won again. Bowman was later hired by the Red Wings, leading them to the Final in 1995, for the first time in 29 years. They lost four straight to the New Jersey Devils.

Two years later, Bowman guided the Red Wings to their first Stanley Cup win in 42 years with a sweep of Philadelphia, which was followed by a sweep of Washington the following spring. The final coaching Cup came in 2002, although Bowman was still a special consultant to the Red Wings when they won in 2008.

"As a coach, winning that first Cup means so much," said Bowman. "It's a great feeling when it finally happens." That last coaching Cup in 2002 was special because Bowman was able to retire doing what few coaches ever accomplish— winning their final game.

"It was nice to be able to go out that way," he said.

Over his 30 years of coaching, Bowman never had a losing record when he coached a full season. He finished with 1,244 regular-season wins and 223 more in the playoffs, both records. His win percentage was .654. Bowman was and remains a student of the game. He was a skilful tactician behind the bench, either matching lines or deftly getting his players away from matchups. He kept everyone on their toes. As the old line goes, Bowman wasn't always loved by his players, except on the day they handed out the bonus cheques.

He was inducted into the Hockey Hall of Fame in 1991.

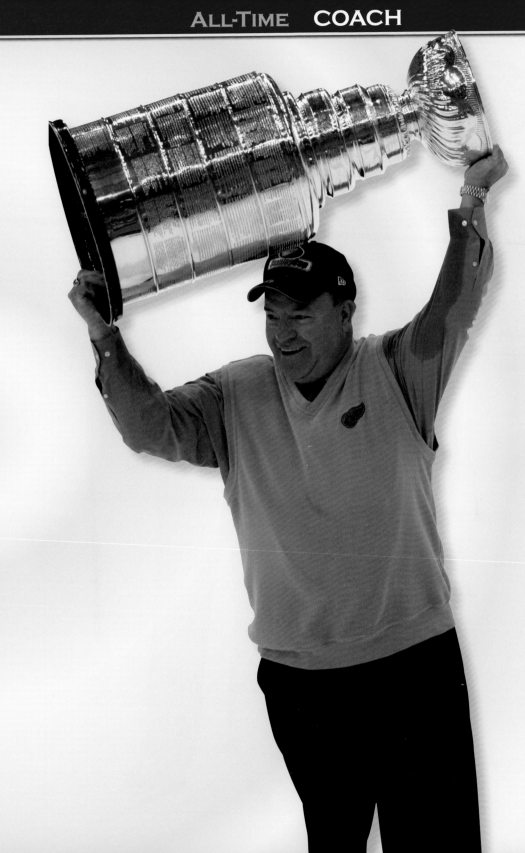

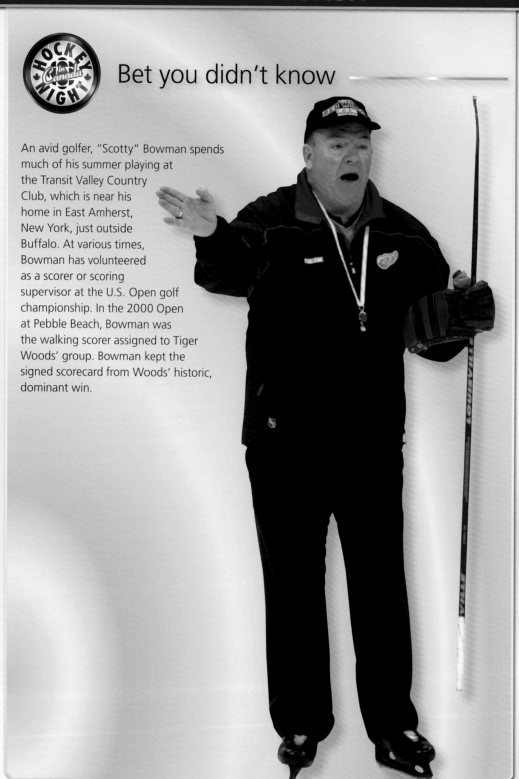

Bet you didn't know

An avid golfer, "Scotty" Bowman spends much of his summer playing at the Transit Valley Country Club, which is near his home in East Amherst, New York, just outside Buffalo. At various times, Bowman has volunteered as a scorer or scoring supervisor at the U.S. Open golf championship. In the 2000 Open at Pebble Beach, Bowman was the walking scorer assigned to Tiger Woods' group. Bowman kept the signed scorecard from Woods' historic, dominant win.

Al Arbour

Al Arbour is living proof you don't have to be a great player to be a great coach. A journeyman defenceman who wore glasses when he played, he carved out a good, but not spectacular, playing career. Arbour managed 626 NHL games over 19 pro seasons, with stops in Detroit, Chicago, Toronto, and finally regular work with the St. Louis Blues when they came into the league in 1967.

He was part of three Stanley Cup-winning teams—one in Chicago in 1961 and two in Toronto in 1962 and 1964. It was his final stop in St. Louis, though, that got Arbour started down the coaching road. He was a steadying influence on the blue line of those expansion Blues teams, coached by Scotty Bowman, that went to the Stanley Cup Final in the first three years of their existence.

Arbour retired early in the 1970–71 season and immediately stepped behind the bench for the departed Bowman. He spent parts of three seasons coaching the Blues before he was named head coach of the New York Islanders in 1973.

Arbour arrived at the same time as a young defenceman named Denis Potvin, and together they eventually built a dynasty on Long Island. In Arbour's second season, he got the Islanders to the playoffs, where they became just the second team ever to overcome a 3–0 playoff series deficit, doing it to the Pittsburgh Penguins in an early round and almost repeating the feat the following round against the Philadelphia Flyers.

While the Islanders were strong in the seasons to follow, they didn't win their first of four consecutive Stanley Cups, just the second club behind Montreal to do so, until 1980.

Arbour won the Jack Adams Award in 1979 and stepped down as coach for the first time after the 1986 playoffs. He returned in 1988 and stayed for five more seasons before retiring in 1994. Arbour finished with 781 career wins in 1,606 games, second only to Bowman.

He was inducted into the Hockey Hall of Fame in 1996.

Bet you didn't know

Al Arbour was invited back by the New York Islanders to stand alongside coach Ted Nolan and coach his 1,500th game as the franchise's head coach. The night was November 3, 2007, and the Isles beat the Pittsburgh Penguins to give Arbour a ceremonial 782nd career win, which is included in the NHL record book for one and all to appreciate.

Hector "Toe" Blake

3

Apparently the old adage that great players don't make good coaches isn't entirely true. Hector "Toe" Blake enjoyed a terrific career with the Montreal Canadiens, scoring 235 goals and 527 points in 577 games over a dozen seasons, which included a Hart Trophy win in his third season.

Blake played on the legendary "Punch Line" with "Rocket" Richard and Elmer Lach, and won two Stanley Cups as a player. He was even captain of the Habs. As good as he was as a player, however, Blake was just as good as a coach, assuming that position with the Canadiens in 1955. He won the Stanley Cup an incredible eight times in 13 seasons behind the bench in Montreal, including five in a row in his first five years.

His record of eight Cup wins as a coach stood until 2002, when Scotty Bowman, who came up through the Canadiens' organization and coached them years after Blake, won his ninth with Detroit.

Blake had a remarkable 82–37 playoff coaching record, with an 18–5 series record, and his team never missed the playoffs during his tenure.

Blake was inducted into the Hockey Hall of Fame as a player in 1966.

Bet you didn't know

Later in his life, after working in a variety of capacities in the Canadiens' front office, "Toe" Blake was diagnosed with Alzheimer's disease. He was eventually placed in a nursing home. He died on May 17, 1995.

Dick Irvin

Dick Irvin had a terrific career as a player, first in junior and senior leagues in Winnipeg and Regina. After a stint in the war, he returned to Regina in the WCHL in 1919, which actually competed for the Stanley Cup. He played a season in Portland then joined the expansion Chicago Black Hawks in 1926 and was named their first captain.

He played three seasons for the Black Hawks in the NHL but was forced into early retirement after he suffered a fractured skull. A few years later, his illustrious coaching career was born. It started in 1928 with the Black Hawks, but the following season he was signed by the Maple Leafs and led them to a Stanley Cup win.

After taking the Leafs to the Final six more times, though not winning, he moved on to Montreal and attained legend status there. He is credited first with saving a struggling franchise and returning it to respectability and then leading it to glory.

Irvin led the Canadiens to three Stanley Cup wins before retiring in 1955, giving way to Toe Blake. Sadly, Irvin passed away a year before he was inducted into the Hockey Hall of Fame in 1958.

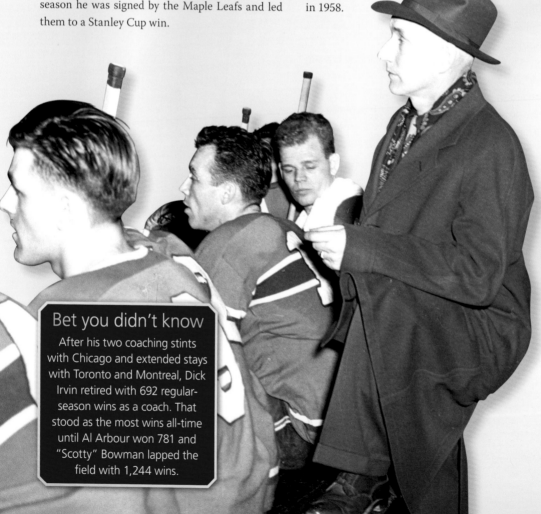

Bet you didn't know

After his two coaching stints with Chicago and extended stays with Toronto and Montreal, Dick Irvin retired with 692 regular-season wins as a coach. That stood as the most wins all-time until Al Arbour won 781 and "Scotty" Bowman lapped the field with 1,244 wins.

Glen Sather

He was a useful journeyman as a player, bouncing around several teams during his 10-year NHL career, but Glen Sather really made his mark as a coach and executive. Sather, who finished his playing career with the Oilers in the WHA in 1977, took over as coach and was involved in the acquisition of Wayne Gretzky from Indianapolis. After the WHA merged with the NHL, Sather added the general manager duties to his portfolio. The Oilers did a terrific job of drafting and developing young talent and, under Sather, built a dynasty.

They advanced to the Stanley Cup Final for the first time in 1983, losing to the New York Islanders who won for a fourth consecutive year. It was a disappointing loss for the Oilers, but one from which they learned what it took to become a champion. And that happened the following spring, when they beat the Islanders for their first of four Cup wins spread over five seasons.

They would add a fifth championship in 1990 with Sather as GM and John Muckler as coach,

a victory that was achieved without Gretzky, who had two years earlier been traded to the Los Angeles Kings.

Sather also had success internationally during those years, coaching Canada to victory in the 1984 Canada Cup. The economic challenges and frustrations in Edmonton, which drove away many of the club's stars over the years, eventually led Sather to New York as GM of the Rangers in the spring of 2000. Sather found himself behind the bench a couple of times on Broadway, but although he has improved financial resources, he hasn't been able to build a champion.

Bet you didn't know

Sather won the Jack Adams award as top coach after the 1985–86 season when the Oilers posted a 56-17-7 record. They had won the Stanley Cup the two previous springs and would win again in the two that followed, but that year the Oilers were upended in the second round, losing in seven games to the Calgary Flames. It is a game and a series that will be remembered for the infamous Steve Smith own-goal that ultimately gave the Flames their margin of victory in the final game.

Fred Shero

As a player, Fred Shero played parts of just three seasons with the New York Rangers, spending most of this time bouncing around the minors. But Shero proved to be not just a student of the game but an innovator as well. He instituted systems, used different training methods, and hired an assistant coach, a first in the NHL. He had a long list of on-ice rules he wanted his players to follow that he put to paper and made them keep in their dressing room stalls. He dared to be different, refusing to follow tradition.

After retiring as a player in 1958, Shero started coaching in junior and minor leagues and was hired by the Philadelphia Flyers in 1971. In five of the seven seasons he was with the Flyers, the team finished with more than 100 points and in four of those seasons had a win percentage over .700.

Those Flyers teams were supremely talented, with the likes of Bernie Parent in goal and Bobby Clarke, Bill Barber, and Reggie Leach up front. But they were known as the "Broad Street Bullies" for a reason. They had a collection of brawlers, such as Dave "The Hammer" Schultz and Don Saleski, useful players who could frighten opponents and contribute quality minutes on the ice.

The Flyers won the Stanley Cup in 1974, with Shero earning the Jack Adams Award, the first expansion team ever to win the big prize. They won the Cup again the following season and lost in the Final to a more skilled Montreal team in 1976.

After leaving the Flyers, Shero went to the Rangers as coach and general manager in 1978–79, leading the Blueshirts to the Cup Final where they lost to Montreal. He stepped down a couple of seasons later and passed away from cancer in November 1990. His son Ray is general manager of the Pittsburgh Penguins and won a Stanley Cup in 2009.

Bet you didn't know

Fred Shero was known for his motivational quotes. Before Game Six of the 1974 Stanley Cup Final, he put the following on the chalkboard in the dressing room: "Win together today and we walk together forever." The Flyers won that night, 1–0, to defeat the Boston Bruins and win their first ever Stanley Cup.

George "Punch" Imlach

In many ways, "Punch" Imlach's NHL coaching career was really launched by himself. After 11 seasons coaching the Quebec Aces, including several seasons with Jean Beliveau as the star player, Imlach spent a year coaching Springfield of the AHL before he was hired by the Toronto Maple Leafs as an assistant general manager. One month on the job and the Leafs fired Billy Reay as coach and Imlach took over as both coach and GM.

Imlach had boldly predicted that the last-place Leafs would make the playoffs, and they did—in spectacular fashion. They were five points behind New York with three games left in the season, but went on to win their games while the Rangers lost theirs. In 1962, the Leafs won the first of three consecutive Stanley Cups with Imlach behind the bench and they won a fourth in 1967, the last in franchise history to date.

Imlach was fired after the 1969 playoffs when the Leafs were swept by Boston in a lopsided series. He went on to join the expansion Buffalo Sabres as coach and GM, behind the bench for the first season and a half. He returned to the Leafs as GM in the late '70s in a bizarre move by the late owner, Harold Ballard, and even coached for 10 games.

Bet you didn't know

One year at the Leafs' training camp, a minor-league defenceman named Don Cherry flattened young prospect Ron Ellis during a scrimmage. That prompted Punch Imlach, who was general manager and coach of the Leafs, to come down from the stands screaming, "Get that fifty-cent hockey player off the ice with that million-dollar player," recalled Cherry in his book *Hockey Stories and Stuff*.

Jack Adams

"Jolly" Jack Adams has several claims to fame, not the least of which is that he is the only person to have his name on the Stanley Cup as a player, coach, and general manager.

Adams' first Cup win was in 1918 with the Toronto Arenas during the first NHL season. He won again in 1927 with a star-studded team in Ottawa.

After he finished playing, Adams was hired as coach of the struggling Detroit Falcons (later named the Red Wings), leading them to back-to-back Cup wins in 1936 and '37. He won another championship in 1943, but only after have suffering bitter disappointment the previous spring when his Red Wings took a 3–0 series lead over the Maple Leafs only to lose the series and Cup in seven games.

He retired as coach after the 1947 season but remained as general manager with the Red Wings, winning another four Stanley Cups. Adams finished with 423 wins over 20 seasons of coaching.

Bet you didn't know

The NHL honoured Jack Adams by annually presenting its coach of the year with the Jack Adams Award. It was first presented to the NHL Broadcasters' Association in 1974 to honour Adams himself and was thereafter presented to the NHL coach judged to have contributed the most to his team's success. The first winner was Philadelphia's Fred Shero. Pat Burns has won the award the most, three times, one each with Montreal, Toronto, and Boston.

Tommy Ivan

Maybe it wasn't hard to discover that Gordie Howe, even while playing in Indianapolis in the minor leagues, had talent. But even a revelation like Howe doesn't guarantee Stanley Cups, and Tommy Ivan, who began his coaching career in the minors while Howe was playing in the Detroit farm system, won Championships.

While with the Detroit Red Wings from 1947 to 1954, he won three Stanley Cups (1950, 1952, and 1954) and earned a reputation for taking talent and making it better. He won another Cup during a long tenure as a general manger with the Chicago Black Hawks (where he also did a little coaching) and earned Hall of Fame honours for developing a team that featured Howe and Terry Sawchuk.

While Ivan was in Detroit he not only won Cups, he led his Wings to first place in the standings seven years in a row. In 1950 and '52, he led the team to the Cup by sweeping a pair of series with Toronto and Montreal, winning the Cup in '52 in just eight games. That team had an amazing seven future members of the Hockey Hall of Fame: Sawchuk, Howe, Ted Lindsay, Alex Delvecchio, Sid Abel, "Red" Kelly, and Marcel Pronovost.

To this day, Ivan is still the winningest coach in All-Star Game history, with a record of 3-0-1. He benefited from a rule that gave him the spot because he regularly took the Red Wings to the Finals, but the record is impressive nonetheless and finishing first seven times in the standings is by no means commonplace.

Bet you didn't know

As a general manager in Chicago, Tommy Ivan was accused of making one of the worst trades of all time, sending Phil Esposito, Ken Hodge, and Fred Stanfield to Boston for Gilles Marotte, Pit Martin, and Jack Norris. That deal eventually made the Bruins a Cup winner, but Ivan was quick to point out that he soon acquired Tony Esposito, one of the greatest goalies of the modern era, and sent Marotte to Los Angeles for Gerry Desjardins. Those deals paid off handsomely for the Black Hawks.

Roger Neilson

For longer than many care to remember, the NHL was a "move-on" league. Players usually moved on to be coaches, coaches often moved on to be general managers. The idea of a "career" coach was not foreign to the NHL, but it was hardly the norm, at least not until Roger Neilson came along.

Neilson was an innovator at every level from juniors to the minors to multiple NHL stops. He was one of the first to bring structured video into training sessions along with updated physical and performance testing. He was also the first to use a headset to communicate with coaches in the press box, using their bird's-eye view of the action to make suggestions as to line changes and strategy.

His NHL career extended through Toronto, Buffalo, Vancouver, Los Angeles, New York (Rangers), Florida, Philadelphia, and Ottawa, and while he never won a Stanley Cup, his methods and teachings had an impact on thousands of players and coaches and forever changed the face of coaching at the NHL level.

Despite not winning a Cup, Neilson had great success and his many stops were a reflection of how much he was valued rather than his "inability" to win the big one. Neilson was a master of the rule book, often using it to his advantage in tight situations and when lobbying referees for calls. His most successful run was a romp with the undermanned Vancouver Canucks, who surprised the hockey pundits with a journey to the Cup Final in 1982, although they lost to a dynastic New York Islanders team.

He was inducted into the Hockey Hall of Fame as a builder in 2002, the same year he was made a member of the Order of Canada. He died in June 2003 from bone cancer, five days after his 69th birthday, and was mourned by millions. Perhaps his best talent was that he could build a good team out of average talent.

Bet you didn't know

Roger Neilson was an innovator, but he also wasn't above trickery. With Peterborough in the OHL, he had a signal that when he tugged on his nose the building supervisor would "unexpectedly" cause a power outage that would delay the game and give his team a chance to regroup. In that same league, his team was once down two men. Realizing no more penalties could be called against his team while the opponent had a two-man advantage, he regularly sent another player over the boards. Each time it created a stoppage in play but no additional penalties— and the stoppages disrupted play and gave his penalty killers time to rest. That rule was quickly changed. Indeed, Neilson caused several rule changes in the OHL and the NHL simply by bending the ones in play in ways others had never considered.

ALL-TIME
GENERAL
MANAGER

1. Sam Pollock
2. Lou Lamoriello
3. Ken Holland
4. Bill Torrey
5. Frank Selke
6. Glen Sather
7. Conn Smythe
8. George "Punch" Imlach
9. Lester Patrick
10. Cliff Fletcher

Sam Pollock

Sam Pollock didn't have an especially long tenure as general manager of the Montreal Canadiens, but it was an incredibly successful and unforgettable one. A native of Montreal, Pollock took over as general manager from the legendary Frank Selke, who ran the club for 18 seasons and was the architect of the great Canadiens teams that won five consecutive Stanley Cups.

Pollock had managed junior teams in the Canadiens system, twice winning the Memorial Cup. He also served as director of player personnel and won a CHL championship with Omaha. He took control of the big club in the spring of 1964 and immediately began establishing his own legendary mark on the team's history. He proved to be a sharp evaluator of talent and a shrewd deal maker, creating a dynasty in Montreal.

During his 14 seasons as general manager, the Canadiens won the Stanley Cup an incredible nine times, including his first two seasons. Under Pollock, the Canadiens' longest Stanley Cup drought was just two seasons. He also created arguably the greatest team ever, certainly the greatest Canadiens team, in the 1976–77 season. That year, the Canadiens set a league record with an impressive 60 wins and just eight losses over 80 games, en route to another Stanley Cup win.

Pollock made some remarkable deals, starting with acquiring goaltender Ken Dryden from the Boston Bruins in 1964 for two players who never played in the NHL. He was also responsible for calling up Dryden late in the 1971 season. Dryden, of course, led the Canadiens to an unexpected Cup victory that spring.

Pollock also dealt for Frank Mahovlich from the Detroit Red Wings, which led to more success, but he made some of his shrewdest moves in the post-expansion era by dealing fringe, aging players for high draft picks.

"Restocking the team was important to us, and we quickly realized that the draft was going to be the major area of importance," said Pollock.

He made a couple of genius moves in 1970 to ensure the Canadiens could potentially get the first pick in the draft—either Guy Lafleur or Marcel Dionne. First, Pollock traded his first-round pick in 1970 and veteran forward Ernie Hicke to the California Golden Seals for their first pick in 1971, which he anticipated would be first overall, and Francois Lacombe.

That next season, when it appeared the Los Angeles Kings might wind up finishing last, meaning the Seals pick he acquired wouldn't be number one overall, Pollock dealt centre Ralph Backstrom to the Kings for a couple of lesser players. Backstrom improved the Kings enough so that they finished ahead of the Seals, giving Pollock the first pick he used to draft Lafleur. That same draft, Pollock selected defenceman Larry Robinson 20th overall. In so many ways he was a visionary.

"People build teams in certain ways," Pollock once said. "I've always traded for futures, not pasts."

Along the way, Pollock also drafted stars such as Steve Shutt and Bob Gainey. He was responsible for replacing Al MacNeil after MacNeil won the Stanley Cup in 1971, and for hiring Scotty Bowman, arguably the greatest coach ever. In eight seasons behind the bench in Montreal, seven of them with Pollock as his boss, Bowman won the Stanley Cup five times, including four consecutive times to end his reign as coach.

"He was a hard worker, had a lot of vision, of course, and was an excellent businessman,"

Bowman once said. "He traded for Mahovlich prior to winning some more Cups and drafted Gainey when most people didn't think it was that good a pick. He had a pretty good handle on junior hockey throughout Canada and he used to scout for us everywhere. Even if they came from colleges or the USA, he was one of the first to take them from there."

It's somewhat forgotten, too, that Pollock was responsible for some of the stars on those great Canadiens teams under Selke in the late 1950s.

Pollock retired as general manager in 1978, the same year he was inducted into the Hockey Hall of Fame. He remained on the Canadiens board and overall, working in the organization, was a part of 11 Stanley Cup championships. Pollock passed away in 2007 at the age of 81.

↻ The 1976 Stanley Cup parade makes its way through downtown Montreal, seemingly an annual ritual during Pollock's reign in the 1970s.

Bet you didn't know

Sam Pollock was the general manager for Team Canada, which won the inaugural Canada Cup in 1976. It is widely believed that Canadian team was the most talented ever, with the likes of Bobby Orr, Darryl Sittler, Robinson, Lafleur, Gainey, Bobby Hull, Denis Potvin, Gilbert Perreault, and Bobby Clarke among others, with Bowman and Don Cherry heading the coaching staff. In total, there were 17 future Hall of Fame players on the roster. Pollock also served as president of the Toronto Blue Jays from 1995 to 2000.

↻ Frank Selke, Sr. (left) with coach Dick Irvin, Sr., was the man most responsible for apprenticing Pollock and helping him become the best GM in NHL history.

The three men most important to Pollock's success as a general manager in Montreal—(left) Guy Lafleur, the number-one draft choice; (top) coach Scotty Bowman; (opposite) goalie Ken Dryden.

Lou Lamoriello

If you believe in anything, especially in having success, the first thing you have to believe in is yourself. Little wonder that after being named president of the New Jersey Devils, Lou Lamoriello, "a college guy" with no experience as an NHL player, coach, or manager at any level, named himself general manager of a franchise largely regarded at the time as a joke.

But Lamoriello wasn't a joke and the Devils, an organization once labelled "Mickey Mouse" by none other than Wayne Gretzky in his prime, immediately began to move forward.

Lamoriello did have stunning success as a coach and athletic director at the college level, so much so that the winner of the Hockey East conference crown receives a trophy that bears his name. But it is in the NHL where the son of a Providence, Rhode Island, restaurant owner has made his enduring mark. A man who believes in putting team above everything else steered the Devils to their first winning season in his first year at the helm—no small accomplishment given that the Devils hadn't posted a winning season since their first year of existence as the Kansas City Scouts.

In Lamoriello's time with New Jersey (starting in 1987), the Devils have made the playoffs in 21 of his 23 seasons, winning three Stanley Cups in four Finals' appearances. He was GM for Team USA at the 1998 Winter Olympics, and he won the Lester Patrick Trophy (1992) for outstanding service to hockey in the United States. In November 2009, he was elected to the Hockey Hall of Fame as a Builder, the only administrative person inducted in a class that brought forth Brett Hull, Brian Leetch, Luc Robitaille, and Steve Yzerman, arguably the Hall's best class of all time.

Bet you didn't know

It was Lamoriello who hired Rick Pitino to coach basketball for Providence College. He also received the UNICO Vince Lombardi Award for Professional Sports Achievement, an Honorary Doctorate Degree from Providence College, and induction into the Providence College Hall of Fame and the New Jersey Sports Hall of Fame. He received the Ellis Island Medal of Honor and was inducted into the Rhode Island Heritage Hall of Fame and the LaSalle Academy (Rhode Island) Hall of Fame. Lamoriello also was a behind-the-scenes player in the settlement of the 2004–05 NHL lockout. He was one of the founders of Hockey East.

3

Ken Holland

The transformation of the Detroit Red Wings (at the time better known as the "Dead Things") didn't start when Ken Holland arrived on the scene; he just took what had been planted and improved upon it until the Wings were universally regarded as the best-run franchise in hockey.

That's no small accomplishment, and there are some critics who believe Lou Lamoriello and the New Jersey Devils deserve something at least akin to equal billing, but taking a good thing and making it better is not always as easy as one would think.

Under Holland, the Wings didn't just win, they won regularly and with style, talent, and a commitment to hockey that was as entertaining as it was successful. Under Holland, the Wings secured talent, especially European talent that the rest of the league largely ignored, overlooked, or didn't invest enough resources in to know it even existed. That's because under Holland, a commitment to winning that started with Jimmy Devallano and was always supported by owners Mike and Marian Illitch, produced extraordinary success.

Holland has won four Stanley Cup championships, the first in 1997 when he was assistant GM and goaltending coach, and three more in 1998, 2002, and 2008 under his leadership. In Holland's era, the Wings have won the Central Division an astounding nine times, the Presidents' Trophy (tops in regular-season play) four times, and, of course, those Cups. From the time Holland was named GM in 1997, his teams have won 493 regular-season games and 67 playoff games. No other NHL franchise has won more.

Bet you didn't know

The record books indicate that Holland was a career minor-league player, but he did suit up in four NHL contests, three of which came with Detroit. He was drafted by the Toronto Maple Leafs in 1985 in the 12th round (the NHL went considerably longer in the drafting of talent back then; he was the 188th player taken overall). He never played a game for the Leafs, but he did play a fourth with the now defunct Hartford Whalers. Though his Wings are known for their commitment to solid offence and stellar defence, Holland was neither a forward nor a defenceman; he was a goaltender.

193

Bill Torrey

The simplest way to measure greatness is to go to the record books. For Bill Torrey, those books say it all. In his early days he turned the Oakland Seals from a sheet of paper into an on-ice success (later marred by its meddlesome owner, Charlie Finley), but it was time spent with the New York Islanders that elevated him and the franchise to its only true success.

Under Torrey, the Islanders went from hapless expansion club to a franchise that won four consecutive Stanley Cups largely because of the talent he assembled, maintained, and improved upon year in, year out. Torrey had a relentless vision of how to build from the ground up, and he steadfastly drafted and developed a core group and then improved it with shrewd acquisitions—without ever cutting in to a core that included the likes of Bryan Trottier, Billy Smith, Denis Potvin, Clark Gillies, and Mike Bossy.

He also made a long-term commitment to coach Al Arbour, a commitment that produced those four Cups, six Patrick Division Championships, and five Stanley Cup Finals appearances. And he did it all from scratch, while working in the shadow of the more highly regarded but eminently less successful New York Rangers.

The aforementioned players all made it to the Hockey Hall of Fame, as did former Islander Pat LaFontaine. Torrey himself was inducted in 1995. Torrey also found success with the Florida Panthers, taking over a newly minted expansion team that made it to the Stanley Cup Final (a losing effort) just three seasons later.

Bet you didn't know

Unlike a lot of GMs of his era, Torrey was a college man, attending St. Lawrence University where he studied business and psychology. He won the Lester Patrick Award for contributions to American hockey and has a banner hanging in his honour in the Nassau County Coliseum. He was also a driving force in bringing NHL hockey to South Florida, lobbying the NHL for a franchise and working the halls at NHL meetings to make it happen. Torrey's Islanders teams went 16–3 in the Finals of those four Cup-winning seasons, including a sweep of a young Edmonton Oilers team in 1983, a team destined for greatness the following season. Since the 1967 expansion, no team except Torrey's Islanders have made it to five straight Stanley Cup Finals.

Frank Selke

You would think if the NHL named a performance trophy to memorialize you that you were a great player. In the case of Frank Selke and the Selke Award (best defensive forward), you would be wrong: Unless you broaden the scope of the word "performance."

Selke made his name off the ice, getting his name on the Stanley Cup an amazing nine times as a managing director to Toronto Maple Leafs owner Conn Smythe (and later with Montreal), helping to build Maple Leaf Gardens, and playing a management role in winning three Cups (1932, 1942, 1945) with the Leafs. He also signed, traded, and developed most of the players of the 1930s and the war years of the '40s for the Leafs.

He had a falling out with Smythe and joined the rival Montreal Canadiens just two months after resigning from the Leafs. There he won Cups in 1953 and a stunning five in a row from 1956–1960, and even those came after a pair of losses to the Red Wings in the Finals in seven-game efforts in 1954 and 1955.

The Leafs enjoyed their longest streak of continuous success under Selke, who duplicated and then surpassed his achievements in Toronto during his time with the Canadiens. In recognition of all that he had accomplished, Selke was elected to the Hockey Hall of Fame in 1960, four years before he retired from the Canadiens. In addition to that honour and the Selke Award in the NHL, his name is attached to a trophy in the Quebec Major Junior Hockey League for gentlemanly play. He's also a member of the Canadian Horse Racing Hall of Fame as a breeder and owner of thoroughbred race horses.

Bet you didn't know

The fallout of a deal that sent Frank Eddolls to the Canadiens in return for the rights to 17-year-old Ted Kennedy (a deal that proved Selke knew more about talent than Conn Smythe) is said to be the reason for the split between Smythe and Selke. Selke eventually left the organization, but the split went deeper than that. Smythe was overseas in the military when that deal was made, but he was also in the war when Selke started booking events other than hockey into the Gardens. The events added quite a bit of money to the bottom line, and that encouraged some members of the board of directors to urge moving Selke ahead of Smythe in terms of franchise operations. Smythe fought that proposal successfully, and Selke moved on to Montreal.

Glen Sather

Glen Sather is better known as "Slats" and best known as the general manager who built the Edmonton Oilers into a dynasty that won five Stanley Cups. Sather made his mark with Edmonton—a mark of greatness. He built the Edmonton dynasty in the mid-1980s and 1990.

He also coached the bulk of those teams that set records for goals scored, won three Presidents Trophies, and was the coach of record for four of those five Cups. As a GM he built a dynasty via shrewd drafting and trades to upgrade the supporting cast around his superstars, led by Wayne Gretzky.

In his first draft, Sather grabbed Paul Coffey, Jari Kurri, and Andy Moog. In his second he acquired Grant Fuhr and Steve Smith. In addition to Mark Messier, they all played a major role in Edmonton championships. (Messier was drafted in 1979 and was already on the team when Sather took over, as was longtime linemate Glenn Anderson.)

After losing in a four-game sweep to the defending Stanley Cup–champion New York Islanders in the 1983 Final, Sather and the team went on to stunning achievements. They won the Cup the following season and three more in the next four years. After Gretzky was traded to Los Angeles, Sather still had a champion-calibre team on his hands.

He added some new players to the mix and his team won yet another Cup in 1990 with John Muckler as coach. As a coach, Sather still has the best winning percentage of any team in NHL history. He also led Team Canada to the 1984 Canada Cup and was general manager of the team that won the World Championship in 1994.

Sather left the Oilers to take over the New York Rangers, but despite a better budget he has yet to find the winning formula in the Big Apple.

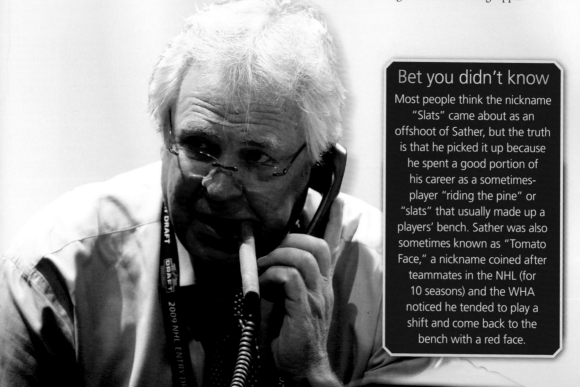

Bet you didn't know

Most people think the nickname "Slats" came about as an offshoot of Sather, but the truth is that he picked it up because he spent a good portion of his career as a sometimes-player "riding the pine" or "slats" that usually made up a players' bench. Sather was also sometimes known as "Tomato Face," a nickname coined after teammates in the NHL (for 10 seasons) and the WHA noticed he tended to play a shift and come back to the bench with a red face.

Conn Smythe

Constantine Falkland Cary Smythe, better known as Conn Smythe, is famous for a quote. It has been paraphrased in many ways, but reputable research suggests that it went like this: "If you can't beat them in the alley, you can't beat them on the ice." He was a legend in the game's formidable Original Six era.

Smythe was a businessman who built Maple Leaf Gardens during the Great Depression. He was the most productive owner of the Maple Leafs and a major in the military. He served in two world wars. He was a successful businessman away from hockey, and a philanthropist of extraordinary renown. Yet it is for his work with the Leafs that

he is best remembered. Smythe has his name on the Stanley Cup 11 times, all of them with his beloved Toronto.

Symthe dabbled in coaching at the amateur and senior levels and briefly headed up the New York Rangers, but his legacy was building the Leafs, their brand, and their building into iconic institutions. Under his leadership, the Leafs won Cups starting in 1932, with the last of his 11 coming in 1967. It is duly noted that the Leafs haven't won a championship since.

In 1965, the NHL attached his name to the trophy that goes to the player judged to be the most valuable in the playoffs. Until the league's divisions were named for geographic regions, his name was also attached to one of the league's divisions. He was inducted into the Hockey Hall of Fame in 1958.

⊂ Smythe with one of his Leafs' stars, Max Bentley.

Bet you didn't know

Like his friend and later rival Frank Selke, Smythe had a passion for horse racing. He owned a stable that claimed some 145 stakes wins over the years. According to legend, Smythe started the Leafs on the road to greatness by purchasing King Clancy from the first edition of the Ottawa Senators. Reportedly, Smythe delivered two players to the Senators, but rumour has it he also paid the Sens $35,000. It was an unheard of sum at the time and it is said to have come from his horse-racing winnings.

8 George "Punch" Imlach

Though it seemed that "Punch" Imlach was around the Toronto Maple Leafs forever, he actually got a relatively late start in his hockey career, joining the club as an assistant GM at the age of 40. From that day forward, however, he wasted no time moving ahead.

A tough taskmaster in the vein of Eddie Shore, for whom Imlach worked in Springfield, Imlach had a reputation for verbally abusing players and denying them the few rights they had. He also had a demonstrated preference for older players, but he found success nonetheless.

Imlach won four Stanley Cups with a tight mixture of veteran players and up-and-coming talent. He was a master trader and usually brought in top talent that kept the Leafs in Cup contention for years. When he finally had a falling out with Toronto ownership, he resurfaced in Buffalo as both a coach (for a time) and the most colourful general manager in franchise history. He did his job, taking the expansion team from a sheet of paper to a playoff participant in three seasons,

and to the Stanley Cup Final (a six-game loss to Philadelphia) in 1975.

Imlach was eventually fired by the Sabres and returned to the Leafs under owner Harold Ballard. That, too, proved to be a controversial time and Imlach again had running feuds with many of his players, notably the iconic Darryl Sittler, whom he tried to trade away (despite Sittler having a no-trade contract).

Heart problems eventually forced "Punch" into retirement but that, too, was controversial.

After his release from hospital for treatment, Imlach returned to the Gardens to find that his parking spot and his job had been given to then-assistant GM Gerry McNamara.

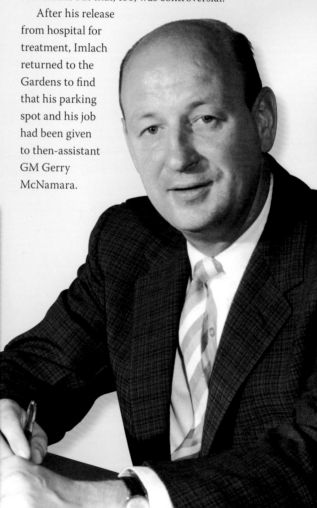

Bet you didn't know

While health and a stormy relationship is said to have led to Imlach's replacement in Buffalo, there was a deeper reason. The Knox family, which owned the team at the time, had contracted with the league to have the Sabres play Moscow Dynamo as part of the first-ever, in-season series between Soviet clubs and the NHL. Like Harold Ballard, Imlach was adamantly opposed to such games and told the Knoxes in no uncertain terms. When that didn't dissuade them, he went down to the Memorial Auditorium office (the building was then being run by the City of Buffalo) and booked the agreed-upon dates for the Russian game for himself. That was too much for the Knoxes, who were immensely loyal to the league. Imlach paid the price.

Lester Patrick

There's a certain irony in the fact that Lester Patrick was born in Canada and had extensive success in his native land, yet is best known for his work with the New York Rangers. It's stranger still that he eventually had a trophy named in his honour, awarded annually to individuals who have advanced the legacy of hockey in the United States.

Talk about your renaissance man.

Patrick was the forerunner of a host of Patricks who have made contributions to hockey. His legacy is all-encompassing in that he was a standout player as an amateur and among the first ever to play in the National Hockey Association, the precursor to the NHL.

He was also famous for building arenas that could produce artificial ice, and he was a legendary administrator of the Pacific Coast Hockey Association, a league that, along with the Western Hockey Association, often challenged eastern rivals for the Stanley Cup.

Still, it was with the New York Rangers that Patrick made his NHL mark, an association that ran from 1926 to 1946 and saw him succeed as a coach, a playing coach, and an administrator. Patrick was general manager when the Rangers won the Cup in 1940, a year that became a derisive chant years later at Madison Square Garden until the Rangers won again in 1994.

Patrick's immense contributions to hockey convinced the league (and especially the Rangers) to arrange for the Lester Patrick Award to recognize others who made contributions to the game in the U.S. Its recipients are a who's who of hockey legends.

He was also the Patrick for whom the Patrick Division was named, prior to the league changing names to reflect geography as opposed to the great names of the past. He has been inducted into the Hockey Hall of Fame, as was his son Lynn and his grandson Craig, both of whom had success as general managers. Another son, "Muzz," was also a standout player and later the GM of the Rangers, while another grandson, Dick, is president of the Washington Capitals and a part owner of that team.

Bet you didn't know

At the age of 44 and well into his coaching career, Lester Patrick donned the pads and played in goal for the Rangers after an injury to netminder Lorne Chabot in the 1928 playoffs. Patrick allowed one goal. The Rangers won that game and eventually beat the Montreal Maroons for the Stanley Cup. It earned him his name on the Cup as both a coach and a player. Patrick also coached the Rangers to another Cup in 1933 though he didn't play a minute in that series. He was inducted into the Hockey Hall of Fame in 1947.

Cliff Fletcher

He learned his craft from the bottom up, working in the Montreal Canadiens organization as a scout and as a manager in Verdun, one of their affiliates at the time. He contributed to the St. Louis Blues as a scout and assistant GM and managed his first NHL team when the freshly minted Atlanta Flames joined the NHL (before leaving for Calgary several years later).

A legendary trader, Fletcher built the Flames into a contending team that won its one and only Stanley Cup championship under his guidance, in 1989, beating the Montreal Canadiens in the Mecca of hockey, the Montreal Forum. During his time with the Flames, Fletcher's team made the playoffs 16 straight times and annually challenged the Edmonton Oilers for the Smythe Division crown.

He built that Flames winner with shrewd trades, including the acquisition of Lanny MacDonald, who scored the Cup-winning goal in 1989, as well as a deal that brought Doug Gilmour to Calgary from St. Louis.

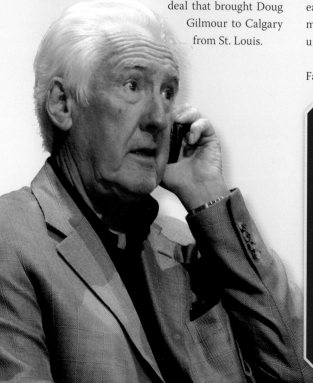

Fletcher eventually joined the Toronto Maple Leafs and quickly rebuilt that failing franchise into a contender with another round of genius trading that earned him the nickname "Trader Cliff." He had his success, however, as his teams made the conference finals in 1993 and 1994. He did it by largely forsaking the draft for trades, including bringing Gilmour and Dave Andreychuk to Toronto, where they quickly became legends.

With Calgary, Fletcher won two Smythe titles and two Campbell Bowls for Western Conference supremacy as well as two President's Trophies. He was the first GM to bring a player from the Soviet Union to the NHL. He also served as GM for Team Canada at the 1981 Canada Cup.

Fletcher went on to Tampa Bay as a senior consultant with then-GM and coach Jacques Demers and later was GM and then consultant to Phoenix when the Coyotes were having some early success. He returned to Toronto as a senior management professional and steered the franchise until Brian Burke arrived to succeed him.

Fletcher was inducted into the Hockey Hall of Fame as a Builder in 2004.

Bet you didn't know

Fletcher was chosen both Man of the Year and Executive of the Year by *Hockey News* in 1993. Much of that was for his hockey success, but Fletcher also fronted the organization during an ugly sex scandal that rocked Maple Leaf Gardens. When the majority of decision makers and the ownership group ran for cover, Fletcher didn't. He faced the media every day with honest answers to difficult questions, a role that earned him undying respect both within the organization and from its critics, including boys who were molested by employees in the Gardens at a time well before Fletcher worked there.

STANLEY CUP CHAMPIONS

1892-93	Montreal AAA	1926-27	Ottawa Senators	1968-69	Montreal Canadiens
1893-94	Montreal AAA	1927-28	New York Rangers	1969-70	Boston Bruins
1894-95	Montreal Victorias	1928-29	Boston Bruins	1970-71	Montreal Canadiens
1895-96	Winnipeg Victorias/	1929-30	Montreal Canadiens	1971-72	Boston Bruins
	Montreal Victorias	1930-31	Montreal Canadiens	1972-73	Montreal Canadiens
1896-97	Montreal Victorias	1931-32	Toronto Maple Leafs	1973-74	Philadelphia Flyers
1897-98	Montreal Victorias	1932-33	New York Rangers	1974-75	Philadelphia Flyers
1898-99	Montreal Victorias/	1933-34	Chicago Black Hawks	1975-76	Montreal Canadiens
	Montreal Shamrocks	1934-35	Montreal Maroons	1976-77	Montreal Canadiens
1899-00	Montreal Shamrocks	1935-36	Detroit Red Wings	1977-78	Montreal Canadiens
1900-01	Winnipeg Victorias	1936-37	Detroit Red Wings	1978-79	Montreal Canadiens
1901-02	Montreal AAA/	1937-38	Chicago Black Hawks	1979-80	New York Islanders
	Winnipeg Victorias	1938-39	Boston Bruins	1980-81	New York Islanders
1902-03	Montreal AAA/Ottawa	1939-40	New York Rangers	1981-82	New York Islanders
	Silver Seven	1940-41	Boston Bruins	1982-83	New York Islanders
1903-04	Ottawa Silver Seven	1941-42	Toronto Maple Leafs	1983-84	Edmonton Oilers
1904-05	Ottawa Silver Seven	1942-43	Detroit Red Wings	1984-85	Edmonton Oilers
1905-06	Ottawa Silver Seven/	1943-44	Montreal Canadiens	1985-86	Montreal Canadiens
	Montreal Wanderers	1944-45	Toronto Maple Leafs	1986-87	Edmonton Oilers
1906-07	Kenora Thistles/	1945-46	Montreal Canadiens	1987-88	Edmonton Oilers
	Montreal Wanderers	1946-47	Toronto Maple Leafs	1988-89	Calgary Flames
1907-08	Montreal Wanderers	1947-48	Toronto Maple Leafs	1989-90	Edmonton Oilers
1908-09	Ottawa Senators	1948-49	Toronto Maple Leafs	1990-91	Pittsburgh Penguins
1909-10	Ottawa Senators/	1949-50	Detroit Red Wings	1991-92	Pittsburgh Penguins
	Montreal Wanderers	1950-51	Toronto Maple Leafs	1992-93	Montreal Canadiens
1910-11	Ottawa Senators	1951-52	Detroit Red Wings	1993-94	New York Rangers
1911-12	Quebec Bulldogs	1952-53	Montreal Canadiens	1994-95	New Jersey Devils
1912-13	Quebec Bulldogs	1953-54	Detroit Red Wings	1995-96	Colorado Avalanche
1913-14	Toronto Blueshirts	1954-55	Detroit Red Wings	1996-97	Detroit Red Wings
1914-15	Vancouver Millionaires	1955-56	Montreal Canadiens	1997-98	Detroit Red Wings
1915-16	Montreal Canadiens	1956-57	Montreal Canadiens	1998-99	Dallas Stars
1916-17	Seattle Metropolitans	1957-58	Montreal Canadiens	1999-00	New Jersey Devils
1917-18	Toronto Arenas	1958-59	Montreal Canadiens	2000-01	Detroit Red Wings
1918-19	no winner—	1959-60	Montreal Canadiens	2001-02	Colorado Avalanche
	flu epidemic	1960-61	Chicago Black Hawks	2002-03	New Jersey Devils
1919-20	Ottawa Senators	1961-62	Toronto Maple Leafs	2003-04	Tampa Bay Lightning
1920-21	Ottawa Senators	1962-63	Toronto Maple Leafs	2004-05	no champion
1921-22	Toronto St. Pats	1963-64	Toronto Maple Leafs	2005-06	Carolina Hurricanes
1922-23	Ottawa Senators	1964-65	Montreal Canadiens	2006-07	Anaheim Ducks
1923-24	Montreal Canadiens	1965-66	Montreal Canadiens	2007-08	Detroit Red Wings
1924-25	Victoria Cougars	1966-67	Toronto Maple Leafs	2008-09	Pittsburgh Penguins
1925-26	Montreal Maroons	1967-68	Montreal Canadiens	2009-10	Chicago Blackhawks

ART ROSS TROPHY

1917-18	Joe Malone	Montreal Canadiens		1964-65	Stan Mikita	Chicago Black Hawks
1918-19	"Newsy" Lalonde	Montreal Canadiens		1965-66	Bobby Hull	Chicago Black Hawks
1919-20	Joe Malone	Quebec Nordiques		1966-67	Stan Mikita	Chicago Black Hawks
1920-21	"Newsy" Lalonde	Montreal Canadiens		1967-68	Stan Mikita	Chicago Black Hawks
1921-22	"Punch" Broadbent	Ottawa Senators		1968-69	Phil Esposito	Boston Bruins
1922-23	"Babe" Dye	Toronto St. Pats		1969-70	Bobby Orr	Boston Bruins
1923-24	Cy Denneny	Ottawa Senators		1970-71	Phil Esposito	Boston Bruins
1924-25	"Babe" Dye	Toronto St. Pats		1971-72	Phil Esposito	Boston Bruins
1925-26	Nels Stewart	Montreal Maroons		1972-73	Phil Esposito	Boston Bruins
1926-27	Bill Cook	New York Rangers		1973-74	Phil Esposito	Boston Bruins
1927-28	Howie Morenz	Montreal Canadiens		1974-75	Bobby Orr	Boston Bruins
1928-29	"Ace" Bailey	Toronto Maple Leafs		1975-76	Guy Lafleur	Montreal Canadiens
1929-30	"Cooney" Weiland	Boston Bruins		1976-77	Guy Lafleur	Montreal Canadiens
1930-31	Howie Morenz	Montreal Canadiens		1977-78	Guy Lafleur	Montreal Canadiens
1931-32	"Busher" Jackson	Toronto Maple Leafs		1978-79	Bryan Trottier	New York Islanders
1932-33	Bill Cook	New York Rangers		1979-80	Marcel Dionne	Los Angeles Kings
1933-34	Charlie Conacher	Toronto Maple Leafs		1980-81	Wayne Gretzky	Edmonton Oilers
1934-35	Charlie Conacher	Toronto Maple Leafs		1981-82	Wayne Gretzky	Edmonton Oilers
1935-36	"Sweeney" Schriner	New York Americans		1982-83	Wayne Gretzky	Edmonton Oilers
1936-37	"Sweeney" Schriner	New York Americans		1983-84	Wayne Gretzky	Edmonton Oilers
1937-38	Gordie Drillon	Toronto Maple Leafs		1984-85	Wayne Gretzky	Edmonton Oilers
1938-39	"Toe" Blake	Montreal Canadiens		1985-86	Wayne Gretzky	Edmonton Oilers
1939-40	Milt Schmidt	Boston Bruins		1986-87	Wayne Gretzky	Edmonton Oilers
1940-41	Bill Cowley	Boston Bruins		1987-88	Mario Lemieux	Pittsburgh Penguins
1941-42	Bryan Hextall	New York Rangers		1988-89	Mario Lemieux	Pittsburgh Penguins
1942-43	Doug Bentley	Chicago Black Hawks		1989-90	Wayne Gretzky	Los Angeles Kings
1943-44	Herb Cain	Boston Bruins		1990-91	Wayne Gretzky	Los Angeles Kings
1944-45	Elmer Lach	Montreal Canadiens		1991-92	Mario Lemieux	Pittsburgh Penguins
1945-46	Max Bentley	Chicago Black Hawks		1992-93	Mario Lemieux	Pittsburgh Penguins
1946-47	Max Bentley	Chicago Black Hawks		1993-94	Wayne Gretzky	Los Angeles Kings
1947-48	Elmer Lach	Montreal Canadiens		1994-95	Jaromir Jagr	Pittsburgh Penguins
1948-49	Roy Conacher	Chicago Black Hawks		1995-96	Mario Lemieux	Pittsburgh Penguins
1949-50	Ted Lindsay	Detroit Red Wings		1996-97	Mario Lemieux	Pittsburgh Penguins
1950-51	Gordie Howe	Detroit Red Wings		1997-98	Jaromir Jagr	Pittsburgh Penguins
1951-52	Gordie Howe	Detroit Red Wings		1998-99	Jaromir Jagr	Pittsburgh Penguins
1952-53	Gordie Howe	Detroit Red Wings		1999-00	Jaromir Jagr	Pittsburgh Penguins
1953-54	Gordie Howe	Detroit Red Wings		2000-01	Jaromir Jagr	Pittsburgh Penguins
1954-55	Bernie Geoffrion	Montreal Canadiens		2001-02	Jarome Iginla	Calgary Flames
1955-56	Jean Beliveau	Montreal Canadiens		2002-03	Peter Forsberg	Colorado Avalanche
1956-57	Gordie Howe	Detroit Red Wings		2003-04	Martin St. Louis	Tampa Bay Lightning
1957-58	Dickie Moore	Montreal Canadiens		2004-05	no winner	
1958-59	Dickie Moore	Montreal Canadiens		2005-06	Joe Thornton	San Jose Sharks
1959-60	Bobby Hull	Chicago Black Hawks		2006-07	Sidney Crosby	Pittsburgh Penguins
1960-61	Bernie Geoffrion	Montreal Canadiens		2007-08	Evgeni Malkin	Pittsburgh Penguins
1961-62	Bobby Hull	Chicago Black Hawks		2008-09	Alex Ovechkin	Washington Capitals
1962-63	Gordie Howe	Detroit Red Wings		2009-10	Henrik Sedin	Vancouver Canucks
1963-64	Stan Mikita	Chicago Black Hawks				

HART TROPHY

1923-24	Frank Nighbor	Ottawa Senators		1967-68	Stan Mikita	Chicago Black Hawks
1924-25	Billy Burch	Hamilton Tigers		1968-69	Phil Esposito	Boston Bruins
1925-26	Nels Stewart	Montreal Maroons		1969-70	Bobby Orr	Boston Bruins
1926-27	Herb Gardiner	Montreal Canadiens		1970-71	Bobby Orr	Boston Bruins
1927-28	Howie Morenz	Montreal Canadiens		1971-72	Bobby Orr	Boston Bruins
1928-29	Roy Worters	New York Americans		1972-73	Bobby Clarke	Philadelphia Flyers
1929-30	Nels Stewart	Montreal Maroons		1973-74	Phil Esposito	Boston Bruins
1930-31	Howie Morenz	Montreal Canadiens		1974-75	Bobby Clarke	Philadelphia Flyers
1931-32	Howie Morenz	Montreal Canadiens		1975-76	Bobby Clarke	Philadelphia Flyers
1932-33	Eddie Shore	Boston Bruins		1976-77	Guy Lafleur	Montreal Canadiens
1933-34	Aurel Joliat	Montreal Canadiens		1977-78	Guy Lafleur	Montreal Canadiens
1934-35	Eddie Shore	Boston Bruins		1978-79	Bryan Trottier	New York Islanders
1935-36	Eddie Shore	Boston Bruins		1979-80	Wayne Gretzky	Edmonton Oilers
1936-37	"Babe" Siebert	Montreal Canadiens		1980-81	Wayne Gretzky	Edmonton Oilers
1937-38	Eddie Shore	Boston Bruins		1981-82	Wayne Gretzky	Edmonton Oilers
1938-39	"Toe" Blake	Montreal Canadiens		1982-83	Wayne Gretzky	Edmonton Oilers
1939-40	Ebbie Goodfellow	Detroit Red Wings		1983-84	Wayne Gretzky	Edmonton Oilers
1940-41	Bill Cowley	Boston Bruins		1984-85	Wayne Gretzky	Edmonton Oilers
1941-42	Tom Anderson	Brooklyn Americans		1985-86	Wayne Gretzky	Edmonton Oilers
1942-43	Bill Cowley	Boston Bruins		1986-87	Wayne Gretzky	Edmonton Oilers
1943-44	"Babe" Pratt	Toronto Maple Leafs		1987-88	Mario Lemieux	Pittsburgh Penguins
1944-45	Elmer Lach	Montreal Canadiens		1988-89	Wayne Gretzky	Edmonton Oilers
1945-46	Max Bentley	Chicago Black Hawks		1989-90	Mark Messier	Edmonton Oilers
1946-47	Maurice Richard	Montreal Canadiens		1990-91	Brett Hull	St. Louis Blues
1947-48	"Buddy" O'Connor	New York Rangers		1991-92	Mark Messier	New York Rangers
1948-49	Sid Abel	Detroit Red Wings		1992-93	Mario Lemieux	Pittsburgh Penguins
1949-50	Chuck Rayner	New York Rangers		1993-94	Sergei Fedorov	Detroit Red Wings
1950-51	Milt Schmidt	Boston Bruins		1994-95	Eric Lindros	Philadelphia Flyers
1951-52	Gordie Howe	Detroit Red Wings		1995-96	Mario Lemieux	Pittsburgh Penguins
1952-53	Gordie Howe	Detroit Red Wings		1996-97	Dominik Hasek	Buffalo Sabres
1953-54	Al Rollins	Chicago Black Hawks		1997-98	Dominik Hasek	Buffalo Sabres
1954-55	Ted Kennedy	Toronto Maple Leafs		1998-99	Jaromir Jagr	Pittsburgh Penguins
1955-56	Jean Beliveau	Montreal Canadiens		1999-00	Chris Pronger	St. Louis Blues
1956-57	Gordie Howe	Detroit Red Wings		2000-01	Joe Sakic	Colorado Avalanche
1957-58	Gordie Howe	Detroit Red Wings		2001-02	Jose Theodore	Montreal Canadiens
1958-59	Andy Bathgate	New York Rangers		2002-03	Peter Forsberg	Colorado Avalanche
1959-60	Gordie Howe	Detroit Red Wings		2003-04	Martin St. Louis	Tampa Bay Lightning
1960-61	Bernie Geoffrion	Montreal Canadiens		2004-05	no winner	
1961-62	Jacques Plante	Montreal Canadiens		2005-06	Joe Thornton	San Jose Sharks
1962-63	Gordie Howe	Detroit Red Wings		2006-07	Sidney Crosby	Pittsburgh Penguins
1963-64	Jean Beliveau	Montreal Canadiens		2007-08	Alex Ovechkin	Washington Capitals
1964-65	Bobby Hull	Chicago Black Hawks		2008-09	Alex Ovechkin	Washington Capitals
1965-66	Bobby Hull	Chicago Black Hawks		2009-10	Henrik Sedin	Vancouver Canucks
1966-67	Stan Mikita	Chicago Black Hawks				

LADY BYNG TROPHY

1924-25	Frank Nighbor	Ottawa Senators
1925-26	Frank Nighbor	Ottawa Senators
1926-27	Billy Burch	New York Americans
1927-28	Frank Boucher	New York Rangers
1928-29	Frank Boucher	New York Rangers
1929-30	Frank Boucher	New York Rangers
1930-31	Frank Boucher	New York Rangers
1931-32	Joe Primeau	Toronto Maple Leafs
1932-33	Frank Boucher	New York Rangers
1933-34	Frank Boucher	New York Rangers
1934-35	Frank Boucher	New York Rangers
1935-36	"Doc" Romnes	Chicago Black Hawks
1936-37	Marty Barry	Detroit Red Wings
1937-38	Gordie Drillon	Toronto Maple Leafs
1938-39	Clint Smith	New York Rangers
1939-40	Bobby Bauer	Boston Bruins
1940-41	Bobby Bauer	Boston Bruins
1941-42	Syl Apps	Toronto Maple Leafs
1942-43	Max Bentley	Chicago Black Hawks
1943-44	Clint Smith	Chicago Black Hawks
1944-45	Bill Mosienko	Chicago Black Hawks
1945-46	"Toe" Blake	Montreal Canadiens
1946-47	Bobby Bauer	Boston Bruins
1947-48	"Buddy" O'Conner	New York Rangers
1948-49	Bill Quackenbush	Detroit Red Wings
1949-50	Edgar Laprade	New York Rangers
1950-51	"Red" Kelly	Detroit Red Wings
1951-52	Sid Smith	Toronto Maple Leafs
1952-53	"Red" Kelly	Detroit Red Wings
1953-54	"Red" Kelly	Detroit Red Wings
1954-55	Sid Smith	Toronto Maple Leafs
1955-56	"Dutch" Reibel	Detroit Red Wings
1956-57	Andy Hebenton	New York Rangers
1957-58	Camille Henry	New York Rangers
1958-59	Alex Delvecchio	Detroit Red Wings
1959-60	Don McKenney	Boston Bruins
1960-61	"Red" Kelly	Toronto Maple Leafs
1961-62	Dave Keon	Toronto Maple Leafs
1962-63	Dave Keon	Toronto Maple Leafs
1963-64	Kenny Wharram	Chicago Black Hawks
1964-65	Bobby Hull	Chicago Black Hawks
1965-66	Alex Delvecchio	Detroit Red Wings
1966-67	Stan Mikita	Chicago Black Hawks
1967-68	Stan Mikita	Chicago Black Hawks
1968-69	Alex Delvecchio	Detroit Black Hawks
1969-70	Phil Goyette	St. Louis Blues
1970-71	John Bucyk	Boston Bruins
1971-72	Jean Ratelle	New York Rangers
1972-73	Gilbert Perreault	Buffalo Sabres
1973-74	John Bucyk	Boston Bruins
1974-75	Marcel Dionne	Detroit Red Wings
1975-76	Jean Ratelle	New York Rangers-Boston Bruins
1976-77	Marcel Dionne	Los Angeles Kings
1977-78	Butch Goring	Los Angeles Kings
1978-79	Bob MacMillan	Atlanta Flames
1979-80	Wayne Gretzky	Edmonton Oilers
1980-81	Rick Kehoe	Pittsburgh Penguins
1981-82	Rick Middleton	Boston Bruins
1982-83	Mike Bossy	New York Islanders
1983-84	Mike Bossy	New York Islanders
1984-85	Jari Kurri	Edmonton Oilers
1985-86	Mike Bossy	New York Islanders
1986-87	Joe Mullen	Calgary Flames
1987-88	Mats Naslund	Montreal Canadiens
1988-89	Joe Mullen	Calgary Flames
1989-90	Brett Hull	St. Louis Blues
1990-91	Wayne Gretzky	Los Angeles Kings
1991-92	Wayne Gretzky	Los Angeles Kings
1992-93	Pierre Turgeon	New York Islanders
1993-94	Wayne Gretzky	Los Angeles Kings
1994-95	Ron Francis	Pittsburgh Penguins
1995-96	Paul Kariya	Anaheim Mighty Ducks
1996-97	Paul Kariya	Anaheim Mighty Ducks
1997-98	Ron Francis	Pittsburgh Penguins
1998-99	Wayne Gretzky	New York Rangers
1999-00	Pavol Demitra	St. Louis Blues
2000-01	Joe Sakic	Colorado Avalanche
2001-02	Ron Francis	Carolina Hurricanes
2002-03	Alexander Mogilny	Toronto Maple Leafs
2003-04	Brad Richards	Tampa Bay Lightning
2004-05	no winner	
2005-06	Pavel Datsuyk	Detroit Red Wings
2006-07	Pavel Datsuyk	Detroit Red Wings
2007-08	Pavel Datsuyk	Detroit Red Wings
2008-09	Pavel Datsuyk	Detroit Red Wings
2009-10	Martin St. Louis	Tampa Bay Lightning

VEZINA TROPHY

1926-27	George Hainsworth	Montreal Canadiens	1970-71	Ed Giacomin	New York Rangers
1927-28	George Hainsworth	Montreal Canadiens		Gilles Villemure	New York Rangers
1928-29	George Hainsworth	Montreal Canadiens	1971-72	Tony Esposito	Chicago Black Hawks
1929-30	"Tiny" Thompson	Boston Bruins		Gary Smith	Chicago Black Hawks
1930-31	Roy Worters	New York Americans	1972-73	Ken Dryden	Montreal Canadiens
1931-32	Charlie Gardiner	Chicago Black Hawks	1973-74	Bernie Parent	Philadelphia Flyers
1932-33	"Tiny" Thompson	Boston Bruins		Tony Esposito	Chicago Black Hawks
1933-34	Charlie Gardiner	Chicago Black Hawks	1974-75	Bernie Parent	Philadelphia Flyers
1934-35	Lorne Chabot	Chicago Black Hawks	1975-76	Ken Dryden	Montreal Canadiens
1935-36	"Tiny" Thompson	Boston Bruins	1976-77	Ken Dryden	Montreal Canadiens
1936-37	Normie Smith	Detroit Red Wings		Michel Larocque	Montreal Canadiens
1937-38	"Tiny" Thompson	Boston Bruins	1977-78	Ken Dryden	Montreal Canadiens
1938-39	Frank Brimsek	Boston Bruins		Michel Larocque	Montreal Canadiens
1939-40	Dave Kerr	New York Rangers	1978-79	Ken Dryden	Montreal Canadiens
1940-41	"Turk" Broda	Toronto Maple Leafs		Michel Larocque	Montreal Canadiens
1941-42	Frank Brimsek	Boston Bruins	1979-80	Bob Sauve	Buffalo Sabres
1942-43	Johnny Mowers	Detroit Red Wings		Don Edwards	Buffalo Sabres
1943-44	Bill Durnan	Montreal Canadiens	1980-81	Richard Sevigny	Montreal Canadiens
1944-45	Bill Durnan	Montreal Canadiens		Dennis Herron	Montreal Canadiens
1945-46	Bill Durnan	Montreal Canadiens		Michel Larocque	Montreal Canadiens
1946-47	Bill Durnan	Montreal Canadiens	1981-82	Billy Smith	New York Islanders
1947-48	"Turk" Broda	Toronto Maple Leafs	1982-83	Pete Peeters	Boston Bruins
1948-49	Bill Durnan	Montreal Canadiens	1983-84	Tom Barrasso	Buffalo Sabres
1949-50	Bill Durnan	Montreal Canadiens	1984-85	Pelle Lindbergh	Philadelphia Flyers
1950-51	Al Rollins	Toronto Maple Leafs	1985-86	John Vanbiesbrouck	New York Rangers
1951-52	Terry Sawchuk	Detroit Red Wings	1986-87	Ron Hextall	Philadelphia Flyers
1952-53	Terry Sawchuk	Detroit Red Wings	1987-88	Grant Fuhr	Edmonton Oilers
1953-54	Harry Lumley	Toronto Maple Leafs	1988-89	Patrick Roy	Montreal Canadiens
1954-55	Terry Sawchuk	Detroit Red Wings	1989-90	Patrick Roy	Montreal Canadiens
1955-56	Jacques Plante	Montreal Canadiens	1990-91	Ed Belfour	Chicago Black Hawks
1956-57	Jacques Plante	Montreal Canadiens	1991-92	Patrick Roy	Montreal Canadiens
1957-58	Jacques Plante	Montreal Canadiens	1992-93	Ed Belfour	Chicago Black Hawks
1958-59	Jacques Plante	Montreal Canadiens	1993-94	Dominik Hasek	Buffalo Sabres
1959-60	Jacques Plante	Montreal Canadiens	1994-95	Dominik Hasek	Buffalo Sabres
1960-61	Johnny Bower	Toronto Maple Leafs	1995-96	Jim Carey	Washington Capitals
1961-62	Jacques Plante	Montreal Canadiens	1996-97	Dominik Hasek	Buffalo Sabres
1962-63	Glenn Hall	Chicago Black Hawks	1997-98	Dominik Hasek	Buffalo Sabres
1963-64	Charlie Hodge	Montreal Canadiens	1998-99	Dominik Hasek	Buffalo Sabres
1964-65	Terry Sawchuk	Toronto Maple Leafs	1999-00	Olaf Kolzig	Washington Capitals
	Johnny Bower	Toronto Maple Leafs	2000-01	Dominik Hasek	Buffalo Sabres
1965-66	"Gump" Worsley	Montreal Canadiens	2001-02	Jose Theodore	Montreal Canadiens
	Charlie Hodge	Montreal Canadiens	2002-03	Martin Brodeur	New Jersey Devils
1966-67	Glenn Hall	Chicago Black Hawks	2003-04	Martin Brodeur	New Jersey Devils
	Denis Dejordy	Chicago Black Hawks	2004-05	no winner	
1967-68	"Gump" Worsley	Montreal Canadiens	2005-06	Miikka Kiprusoff	Calgary Flames
	Rogie Vachon	Montreal Canadiens	2006-07	Martin Brodeur	New Jersey Devils
1968-69	Jacques Plante	St. Louis Blues	2007-08	Martin Brodeur	New Jersey Devils
	Glenn Hall	St. Louis Blues	2008-09	Tim Thomas	Boston Bruins
1969-70	Tony Esposito	Chicago Black Hawks	2009-10	Ryan Miller	Buffalo Sabres

APPENDIX

CALDER MEMORIAL TROPHY

1932-33	Carl Voss	Detroit Red Wings
1933-34	Russ Blinco	Montreal Maroons
1934-35	"Sweeney" Schriner	New York Americans
1935-36	Mike Karakas	Chicago Black Hawks
1936-37	Syl Apps	Toronto Maple Leafs
1937-38	"Cully" Dahlstrom	Chicago Black Hawks
1938-39	Frank Brimsek	Boston Bruins
1939-40	Kilby MacDonald	New York Rangers
1940-41	John Quilty	Montreal Canadiens
1941-42	Grant Warwick	New York Rangers
1942-43	Gaye Stewart	Toronto Maple Leafs
1943-44	Gus Bodnar	Toronto Maple Leafs
1944-45	Frank McCool	Toronto Maple Leafs
1945-46	Edgar Laprade	New York Rangers
1946-47	Howie Meeker	Toronto Maple Leafs
1947-48	Jim McFadden	Detroit Red Wings
1948-49	Pentti Lund	New York Rangers
1949-50	Jack Gelineau	Boston Bruins
1950-51	Terry Sawchuk	Detroit Red Wings
1951-52	Bernie Geoffrion	Montreal Canadiens
1952-53	"Gump" Worsley	New York Rangers
1953-54	Camille Henry	New York Rangers
1954-55	Ed Litzenberger	Chicago Black Hawks
1955-56	Glenn Hall	Detroit Red Wings
1956-57	Larry Regan	Boston Bruins
1957-58	Frank Mahovlich	Toronto Maple Leafs
1958-59	Ralph Backstrom	Montreal Canadiens
1959-60	Bill Hay	Chicago Black Hawks
1960-61	Dave Keon	Toronto Maple Leafs
1961-62	Bobby Rousseau	Montreal Canadiens
1962-63	Kent Douglas	Toronto Maple Leafs
1963-64	Jacques Laperriere	Montreal Canadiens
1964-65	Roger Crozier	Detroit Red Wings
1965-66	Brit Selby	Toronto Maple Leafs
1966-67	Bobby Orr	Boston Bruins
1967-68	Derek Sanderson	Boston Bruins
1968-69	Danny Grant	Minnesota North Stars
1969-70	Tony Esposito	Chicago Black Hawks
1970-71	Gilbert Perreault	Buffalo Sabres
1971-72	Ken Dryden	Montreal Canadiens
1972-73	Steve Vickers	New York Rangers
1973-74	Denis Potvin	New York Islanders
1974-75	Eric Vail	Atlanta Flames
1975-76	Bryan Trottier	New York Islanders
1976-77	Willi Plett	Atlanta Flames
1977-78	Mike Bossy	New York Islanders
1978-79	Bobby Smith	Minnesota North Stars
1979-80	Raymond Bourque	Boston Bruins
1980-81	Peter Stastny	Quebec Nordics
1981-82	Dale Hawerchuk	Winnipeg Jets
1982-83	Steve Larmer	Chicago Black Hawks
1983-84	Tom Barrasso	Buffalo Sabres
1984-85	Mario Lemieux	Pittsburgh Penguins
1985-86	Gary Suter	Calgary Flames
1986-87	Luc Robitaille	Los Angeles Kings
1987-88	Joe Nieuwendyk	Calgary Flames
1988-89	Brian Leetch	New York Rangers
1989-90	Sergei Makarov	Calgary Flames
1990-91	Ed Belfour	Chicago Black Hawks
1991-92	Pavel Bure	Vancouver Canucks
1992-93	Teemu Selanne	Winnipeg Jets
1993-94	Martin Brodeur	New Jersey Devils
1994-95	Peter Forsberg	Quebec Nordiques
1995-96	Daniel Alfredsson	Ottawa Senators
1996-97	Bryan Berard	New York Islanders
1997-98	Sergei Samsonov	Boston Bruins
1998-99	Chris Drury	Colorado Avalanche
1999-00	Scott Gomez	New Jersey Devils
2000-01	Evgeni Nabokov	San Jose Sharks
2001-02	Danny Heatley	Atlanta Thrashers
2002-03	Barret Jackman	St. Louis Blues
2003-04	Andrew Raycroft	Boston Bruins
2004-05	no winner	
2005-06	Alex Ovechkin	Washington Capitals
2006-07	Evgeni Malkin	Pittsburgh Penguins
2007-08	Patrick Kane	Chicago Blackhawks
2008-09	Steve Mason	Columbus Blue Jackets
2009-10	Tyler Myers	Buffalo Sabres

JAMES NORRIS TROPHY

1953-54	"Red" Kelly	Detroit Red Wings	
1954-55	Doug Harvey	Montreal Canadiens	
1955-56	Doug Harvey	Montreal Canadiens	
1956-57	Doug Harvey	Montreal Canadiens	
1957-58	Doug Harvey	Montreal Canadiens	
1958-59	Tom Johnson	Montreal Canadiens	
1959-60	Doug Harvey	Montreal Canadiens	
1960-61	Doug Harvey	Montreal Canadiens	
1961-62	Doug Harvey	Montreal Canadiens	
1962-63	Pierre Pilote	Chicago Black Hawks	
1963-64	Pierre Pilote	Chicago Black Hawks	
1964-65	Pierre Pilote	Chicago Black Hawks	
1965-66	Jacques Laperriere	Montreal Canadiens	
1966-67	Harry Howell	New York Rangers	
1967-68	Bobby Orr	Boston Bruins	
1968-69	Bobby Orr	Boston Bruins	
1969-70	Bobby Orr	Boston Bruins	
1970-71	Bobby Orr	Boston Bruins	
1971-72	Bobby Orr	Boston Bruins	
1972-73	Bobby Orr	Boston Bruins	
1973-74	Bobby Orr	Boston Bruins	
1974-75	Bobby Orr	Boston Bruins	
1975-76	Denis Potvin	New York Islanders	
1976-77	Larry Robinson	Montreal Canadiens	
1977-78	Denis Potvin	New York Islanders	
1978-79	Denis Potvin	New York Islanders	
1979-80	Larry Robinson	Montreal Canadiens	
1980-81	Randy Carlyle	Pittsburgh Penguins	
1981-82	Doug Wilson	Chicago Black Hawks	
1982-83	Rod Langway	Washington Capitals	
1983-84	Rod Langway	Washington Capitals	
1984-85	Paul Coffey	Edmonton Oilers	
1985-86	Paul Coffey	Edmonton Oilers	
1986-87	Raymond Bourque	Boston Bruins	
1987-88	Raymond Bourque	Boston Bruins	
1988-89	Chris Chelios	Montreal Canadiens	
1989-90	Raymond Bourque	Boston Bruins	
1990-91	Raymond Bourque	Boston Bruins	
1991-92	Brian Leetch	New York Rangers	
1992-93	Chris Chelios	Chicago Black Hawks	
1993-94	Raymond Bourque	Boston Bruins	
1994-95	Paul Coffey	Detroit Red Wings	
1995-96	Chris Chelios	Chicago Black Hawks	
1996-97	Brian Leetch	New York Rangers	
1997-98	Rob Blake	Los Angeles Kings	
1998-99	Al MacInnis	St. Louis Blues	
1999-00	Chris Pronger	St. Louis Blues	
2000-01	Nicklas Lidstrom	Detroit Red Wings	
2001-02	Nicklas Lidstrom	Detroit Red Wings	
2002-03	Nicklas Lidstrom	Detroit Red Wings	
2003-04	Scott Niedermayer	New Jersey Devils	
2004-05	no winner		
2005-06	Nicklas Lidstrom	Detroit Red Wings	
2006-07	Nicklas Lidstrom	Detroit Red Wings	
2007-08	Nicklas Lidstrom	Detroit Red Wings	
2008-09	Zdeno Chara	Boston Bruins	
2009-10	Duncan Keith	Chicago Blackhawks	

CONN SMYTHE TROPHY

1964-65	Jean Beliveau	Montreal Canadiens	1987-88	Wayne Gretzky	Edmonton Oilers
1965-66	Roger Crozier	Detroit Red Wings	1988-89	Al MacInnis	Calgary Flames
1966-67	Dave Keon	Toronto Maple Leafs	1989-90	Bill Ranford	Edmonton Oilers
1967-68	Glenn Hall	St. Louis Blues	1990-91	Mario Lemieux	Pittsburgh Penguins
1968-69	Serge Savard	Montreal Canadiens	1991-92	Mario Lemieux	Pittsburgh Penguins
1969-70	Bobby Orr	Boston Bruins	1992-93	Patrick Roy	Montreal Canadiens
1970-71	Ken Dryden	Montreal Canadiens	1993-94	Brian Leetch	New York Rangers
1971-72	Bobby Orr	Boston Bruins	1994-95	Claude Lemieux	New Jersey Devils
1972-73	Yvan Cournoyer	Montreal Canadiens	1995-96	Joe Sakic	Colorado Avalanche
1973-74	Bernie Parent	Philadelphia Flyers	1996-97	Mike Vernon	Detroit Red Wings
1974-75	Bernie Parent	Philadelphia Flyers	1997-98	Steve Yzerman	Detroit Red Wings
1975-76	Reg Leach	Philadelphia Flyers	1998-99	Joe Nieuwendyk	Dallas Stars
1976-77	Guy Lafleur	Montreal Canadiens	1999-00	Scott Stevens	New Jersey Devils
1977-78	Larry Robinson	Montreal Canadiens	2000-01	Patrick Roy	Colorado Avalanche
1978-79	Bob Gainey	Montreal Canadiens	2001-02	Nicklas Lidstrom	Detroit Red Wings
1979-80	Bryan Trottier	New York Islanders	2002-03	J-S Giguere	Mighty Ducks of Anaheim
1980-81	Butch Goring	New York Islanders	2003-04	Brad Richards	Tampa Bay Lightning
1981-82	Mike Bossy	New York Islanders	2004-05	no winner	
1982-83	Billy Smith	New York Islanders	2005-06	Cam Ward	Carolina Hurricanes
1983-84	Mark Messier	Edmonton Oilers	2006-07	Scott Niedermayer	Anaheim Ducks
1984-85	Wayne Gretzky	Edmonton Oilers	2007-08	Henrik Zetterberg	Detroit Red Wings
1985-86	Patrick Roy	Montreal Canadiens	2008-09	Evgeni Malkin	Pittsburgh Penguins
1986-87	Ron Hextall	Philadelphia Flyers	2009-10	Jonathan Toews	Chicago Blackhawks

BILL MASTERTON TROPHY

1967-68	Claude Provost	Montreal Canadiens
1968-69	Ted Hampson	Oakland Seals
1969-70	Pit Martin	Chicago Black Hawks
1970-71	Jean Ratelle	New York Rangers
1971-72	Bobby Clarke	Philadelphia Flyers
1972-73	Lowell MacDonald	Pittsburgh Penguins
1973-74	Henri Richard	Montreal Canadiens
1974-75	Don Luce	Buffalo Sabres
1975-76	Rod Gilbert	New York Rangers
1976-77	Ed Westfall	New York Islanders
1977-78	Butch Goring	Los Angeles Kings
1978-79	Serge Savard	Montreal Canadiens
1979-80	Al MacAdam	Minnesota North Stars
1980-81	Blake Dunlop	St. Louis Blues
1981-82	Glenn Resch	Colorado Rockies
1982-83	Lanny McDonald	Calgary Flames
1983-84	Brad Park	Detroit Red Wings
1984-85	Anders Hedberg	New York Rangers
1985-86	Charlie Simmer	Boston Bruins
1986-87	Doug Jarvis	Hartford Whalers
1987-88	Bob Bourne	Los Angeles Kings
1988-89	Tim Kerr	Philadelphia Flyers
1989-90	Gord Kluzak	Boston Bruins
1990-91	Dave Taylor	Los Angeles Kings
1991-92	Mark Fitzpatrick	New York Islanders
1992-93	Mario Lemieux	Pittsburgh Penguins
1993-94	Cam Neely	Boston Bruins
1994-95	Pat LaFontaine	Buffalo Sabres
1995-96	Gary Roberts	Calgary Flames
1996-97	Tony Granato	San Jose Sharks
1997-98	Jamie McLennan	St. Louis Blues
1998-99	John Cullen	Tampa Bay Lightning
1999-00	Ken Daneyko	New Jersey Devils
2000-01	Adam Graves	New York Rangers
2001-02	Saku Koivu	Montreal Canadiens
2002-03	Steve Yzerman	Detroit Red Wings
2003-04	Bryan Berard	Chicago Blackhawks
2004-05	no winner	
2005-06	Teemu Selanne	Anaheim Ducks
2006-07	Phil Kessel	Boston Bruins
2007-08	Jason Blake	Toronto Maple Leafs
2008-09	Steve Sullivan	Nashville Predators
2009-10	Jose Theodore	Washington Capitals

JACK ADAMS AWARD

1973-74	Fred Shero	Philadelphia Flyers
1974-75	Bob Pulford	Los Angeles Kings
1975-76	Don Cherry	Boston Bruins
1976-77	"Scotty" Bowman	Montreal Canadiens
1977-78	Bobby Kromm	Detroit Red Wings
1978-79	Al Arbour	New York Islanders
1979-80	Pat Quinn	Philadelphia Flyers
1980-81	Red Berenson	St. Louis Blues
1981-82	Tom Watt	Winnipeg Jets
1982-83	Orval Tessier	Chicago Black Hawks
1983-84	Bryan Murray	Washington Capitals
1984-85	Mike Keenan	Philadelphia Flyers
1985-86	Glen Sather	Edmonton Oilers
1986-87	Jacques Demers	Detroit Red Wings
1987-88	Jacques Demers	Detroit Red Wings
1988-89	Pat Burns	Montreal Canadiens
1989-90	Bob Murdoch	Winnipeg Jets
1990-91	Brian Sutter	St. Louis Blues
1991-92	Pat Quinn	Vancouver Canucks
1992-93	Pat Burns	Toronto Maple Leafs
1993-94	Jacques Lemaire	New Jersey Devils
1994-95	Marc Crawford	Quebec Nordiques
1995-96	"Scotty" Bowman	Detroit Red Wings
1996-97	Ted Nolan	Buffalo Sabres
1997-98	Pat Burns	Boston Bruins
1998-99	Jacques Martin	Ottawa Senators
1999-00	Joel Quenneville	St. Louis Blues
2000-01	Bill Barber	Philadelphia Flyers
2001-02	Bob Francis	Phoenix Coyotes
2002-03	Jacques Lemaire	Minnesota Wild
2003-04	John Tortorella	Tampa Bay Lightning
2004-05	no winner	
2005-06	Lindy Ruff	Buffalo Sabres
2006-07	Alain Vigneault	Vancouver Canucks
2007-08	Bruce Boudreau	Washington Capitals
2008-09	Claude Julien	Boston Bruins
2009-10	Dave Tippett	Phoenix Coyotes

APPENDIX

LESTER B. PEARSON AWARD

1970-71	Phil Esposito	Boston Bruins
1971-72	Jean Ratelle	New York Rangers
1972-73	Bobby Clarke	Philadelphia Flyers
1973-74	Phil Esposito	Boston Bruins
1974-75	Bobby Orr	Boston Bruins
1975-76	Guy Lafleur	Montreal Canadiens
1976-77	Guy Lafleur	Montreal Canadiens
1977-78	Guy Lafleur	Montreal Canadiens
1978-79	Marcel Dionne	Los Angeles Kings
1979-80	Marcel Dionne	Los Angeles Kings
1980-81	Mike Liut	St. Louis Blues
1981-82	Wayne Gretzky	Edmonton Oilers
1982-83	Wayne Gretzky	Edmonton Oilers
1983-84	Wayne Gretzky	Edmonton Oilers
1984-85	Wayne Gretzky	Edmonton Oilers
1985-86	Mario Lemieux	Pittsburgh Penguins
1986-87	Wayne Gretzky	Edmonton Oilers
1987-88	Mario Lemieux	Pittsburgh Penguins
1988-89	Steve Yzerman	Detroit Red Wings
1989-90	Mark Messier	Edmonton Oilers
1990-91	Brett Hull	St. Louis Blues
1991-92	Mark Messier	New York Rangers
1992-93	Mario Lemieux	Pittsburgh Penguins
1993-94	Sergei Fedorov	Detroit Red Wings
1994-95	Eric Lindros	Philadelphia Flyers
1995-96	Mario Lemieux	Pittsburgh Penguins
1996-97	Dominik Hasek	Buffalo Sabres
1997-98	Dominik Hasek	Buffalo Sabres
1998-99	Jaromir Jagr	Pittsburgh Penguins
1999-00	Jaromir Jagr	Pittsburgh Penguins
2000-01	Joe Sakic	Colorado Avalanche
2001-02	Jarome Iginla	Calgary Flames
2002-03	Markus Naslund	Vancouver Canucks
2003-04	Martin St. Louis	Tampa Bay Lightning
2004-05	no winner	
2005-06	Jaromir Jagr	New York Rangers
2006-07	Sidney Crosby	Pittsburgh Penguins
2007-08	Alex Ovechkin	Washington Capitals
2008-09	Alex Ovechkin	Washington Capitals

re-named **Ted Lindsay Award**

2009-10	Alex Ovechkin	Washington Capitals

FRANK J. SELKE TROPHY

1977-78	Bob Gainey	Montreal Canadiens
1978-79	Bob Gainey	Montreal Canadiens
1979-80	Bob Gainey	Montreal Canadiens
1980-81	Bob Gainey	Montreal Canadiens
1981-82	Steve Kasper	Boston Bruins
1982-83	Bobby Clarke	Pittsburgh Penguins
1983-84	Doug Jarvis	Washington Capitals
1984-85	Craig Ramsay	Buffalo Sabres
1985-86	Troy Murray	Chicago Black Hawks
1986-87	Dave Poulin	Philadelphia Flyers
1987-88	Guy Carbonneau	Montreal Canadiens
1988-89	Guy Carbonneau	Montreal Canadiens
1989-90	Rick Meagher	St. Louis Blues
1990-91	Dirk Graham	Chicago Black Hawks
1991-92	Guy Carbonneau	Montreal Canadiens
1992-93	Doug Gilmour	Toronto Maple Leafs
1993-94	Sergei Fedorov	Detroit Red Wings
1994-95	Ron Francis	Pittsburgh Penguins
1995-96	Sergei Fedorov	Detroit Red Wings
1996-97	Michael Peca	Buffalo Sabres
1997-98	Jere Lehtinen	Dallas Stars
1998-99	Jere Lehtinen	Dallas Stars
1999-00	Steve Yzerman	Detroit Red Wings
2000-01	John Madden	New Jersey Devils
2001-02	Michael Peca	New York Islanders
2002-03	Jere Lehtinen	Dallas Stars
2003-04	Kris Draper	Detroit Red Wings
2004-05	no winner	
2005-06	Rod Brind'Amour	Carolina Hurricanes
2006-07	Rod Brind'Amour	Carolina Hurricanes
2007-08	Pavel Datsyuk	Detroit Red Wings
2008-09	Pavel Datsyuk	Detroit Red Wings
2009-10	Pavel Datsyuk	Detroit Red Wings

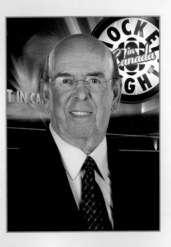

Dean Brown has been the voice of the Ottawa Senators on both radio and television since hockey returned to the Nation's Capital in 1992. He has done play-by-play of Senators games on Rogers Sportsnet since 1998 and has also been a regular on CBC's *Hockey Night in Canada* since 1998, though not just calling Senators games. Brown was previously a news anchor in Winnipeg and London before moving to Ottawa as a sports announcer in 1983, and he was the play-by-play voice of the Canadian Football League's Ottawa Rough Riders.

Cassie Campbell took part in three Olympic Winter Games and was the captain of the Canadian women's hockey team during the 2002 Olympics in Salt Lake City, where she led her team to a gold-medal victory. Four years later, she reprised her role as captain and won gold again at the 2006 Olympics in Turin, Italy. She competed in seven International Ice Hockey Federation World Women's Championships and nine Four Nations Cups among her many prestigious events, earning 21 medals in total (17 gold medals and four silver medals). Campbell retired from competitive hockey in August 2006, and joined CBC's *Hockey Night in Canada* the same year.

A front-line player on CBC's *Hockey Night in Canada* for 37 years, **Bob Cole** was inducted into the Hockey Hall of Fame in 1996 when he was named the winner of the Foster Hewitt Memorial Award for excellence in hockey broadcasting. During the Team Canada-Soviet Union Summit Series in 1972, Hewitt made the famous call of Paul Henderson's winning goal on television—while Cole did the same on radio.

The next year, HNIC producer Ralph Mellanby asked Cole to join fellow play-by-play announcers Danny Gallivan and Bill Hewitt. In 1985, Cole and colour commentator Harry Neale joined forces and became one of hockey's strongest on-air teams.

Former NHL All-Star defenceman **Garry Galley** works as an analyst on CBC's *Hockey Night in Canada's* regular season tripleheader broadcasts and on Stanley Cup playoff telecasts. In addition, Galley co-hosts the daily "More On Sports" afternoon radio show on the Team 1200 in Ottawa and works as an analyst for Rogers Sportsnet NHL regional game broadcasts. A 17-year veteran of the NHL, Galley was drafted in 1983 and played 1,149 games for six different teams: Los Angeles, Washington, Boston, Philadelphia, Buffalo, and the New York Islanders. The two-time NHL All-Star also represented Canada twice in the IIHF World Championships and was nominated on two occasions for the Bill Masterton Memorial Trophy for dedication and perseverance to the game.

Kelly Hrudey works as an analyst for CBC's *Hockey Night in Canada*. Hrudey's segment "Behind the Mask" became a regular feature starting in the 1999 playoffs. A former NHL goalie, Hrudey also works as a host on CBC's *Hockey Night in Canada* radio on Sirius Satellite. During his 15-year NHL career as a goalie with the New York Islanders (six years), Los Angeles Kings (seven years), and San Jose Sharks (two years), the former Medicine Hat Tiger compiled a record of 271-265-88, with a goals-against average of 3.43 and 16 shutouts.

Hockey broadcasting veteran **Jim Hughson** began his impressive NHL broadcasting career in October 1979. His 31-year storied career includes calling Wayne Gretzky's final game in Canada at the Corel Centre in April 1999, and calling thousands of NHL games. A Gemini Award winner in 2004 for sports play-by-play, Hughson has also been part of several national baseball broadcasts, including the 1992 and 1993 Toronto Blue Jays' Division Championship series.

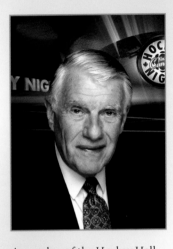

A member of the Hockey Hall of Fame as a broadcaster, **Dick Irvin** has been part of CBC's hockey broadcasting team for 40 years. To viewers of CBC's *Hockey Night in Canada*, the Regina, Saskatchewan, native is best known for his coverage of Montreal Canadiens games. In fact, Irvin travelled with the Habs for more than 30 years as their radio broadcaster and has covered close to 3,000 NHL games on TV and radio. In 1988, Irvin received the Foster Hewitt Memorial Award for excellence in hockey broadcasting. Along with his award-winning work on the airwaves, he is also an accomplished author. His books include *The Habs: Behind the Bench* and *In the Crease: Goaltenders Look at Life in the NHL*.

Northern Ontario native **Pierre LeBrun**, commentator on CBC's *Hockey Night in Canada's* popular segment "Satellite Hotstove," has covered the NHL since the 1995–96 season. He has also been a regular correspondent with espn.com since 2008. Hired by the Canadian Press national news agency in 1995, LeBrun also added television broadcast responsibilities to his resume, joining The Score television network in 2003 and the "Satellite Hotstove" panel in 2005. LeBrun received Sports Media Canada's award for outstanding sports writing in 2005 as well as CP's President's Award. LeBrun covered six straight men's world hockey championships in Europe from 2000 to 2005, as well as the 2002, 2006, and 2010 Olympic Winter Games, and the yearly Stanley Cup finals.

Gemini Award-winner **Mark Lee** is a play-by-play announcer for CBC's *Hockey Night in Canada*. He has also covered 11 Olympic Games on the CBC, and many fans will know his work for the CFL on CBC. Mark also calls play by play for all of CBC's track and field coverage. Born in Calgary, the Carleton University graduate got his start in radio at CKOY-CKBY FM while earning a degree in journalism. Lee's documentary reporting earned him two Actra Awards as Best Sportscaster. Lee's television breakthrough came in 1991, when he was assigned to follow Michael Smith, the defending Commonwealth Games decathlon champion. In 1994, he won a Gemini Award for *The Spirit of the Game*, a three-part documentary on hockey.

Jeff Marek joined CBC's *Hockey Night in Canada* in 2007 as Host of CBC's *Hockey Night in Canada* on Sirius Radio. During select games throughout the season, Marek works as a rinkside reporter for HNIC and also appears on the I-Desk with Scott Morrison hosting live chats with hockey fans across the country. A 14-year veteran of talk radio, Marek began his professional career in 1995 at the Fan 590 in Toronto. He worked at AM 640 Toronto Radio starting in 2000, hosting "The Jeff Marek Show," a nightly open-line talk show, while working as the station's morning news anchor. He quickly became the director of sports news and joined host Bill Watters on "Leafs' Lunch." Marek regularly appears on CBC Newsworld and was one of the original writers for The Sports Network's (TSN) "Off The Record." Marek was also a regular guest panelist.

Mike Milbury has been with CBC's *Hockey Night in Canada* for three years, bringing more than 30 years of experience as an NHL defenceman, coach, executive, and broadcaster to his role. Although a relative newcomer to the broadcast world, his extensive work as an analyst with networks in both Canada and the United States has enabled him to solidify his reputation as a dependable and experienced voice in the NHL. The former Boston Bruin provides viewers with firsthand knowledge of the game and the business of professional hockey. After his career as an NHL player, Milbury moved behind the bench for two seasons with the Bruins, leading them to the best regular-season record in the NHL and to the Stanley Cup Final during the 1989-90 season. Milbury moved to the New York Islanders organization in 1995.

Scott Oake joined the CBC in 1974. Best known for his work as host of CBC's *Hockey Night in Canada*'s western broadcasts as well as host of "After Hours," Oake's role as the alpine skiing commentator at Turin 2006 marked the tenth Olympiad he has covered during his storied career. Oake also hosted the CFL on CBC broadcasts for eight years, from 1988 to 1996. In 2004, he hosted the hockey docudrama "Making the Cut." From the NHL's boardrooms to the players' dressing room, Oake has interviewed some of the game's brightest and most intriguing stars. In 2003, his interview with Brett Hull earned him a Gemini Award for Best Host or Interviewer in a Sports Program or Broadcast.

The

dar

on

key experts

Scott Morrison.

works closely with

Hockey Night in Canada

vide story content.

g as

roadcast

Simpson

ups with

88 and 1990,

to hold the

of being the last

ore 50 goals in one

6 goals in 1987–88).

Ho

Andrew Podnieks is the author of some 55 books on hockey, most recently *Retired Numbers*, *Superstitions*, and the best-selling *Canadian Gold 2010*. Additionally, he has worked with the IIHF, Hockey Canada, the Hockey Hall of Fame, and Canada's Sports Hall of Fame. Podnieks has created media guides for all major IIHF events—the Olympics, World Championships, World Women's Championships, and World Junior (U20) Championships. He writes extensively for www.IIHF.com on a regular basis and has covered three Olympics and nine World Championships among his many assignments for hockey's governing body of international hockey. His website is www.andrewpodnieks.com.

Two-time Stanley Cup Champion **Craig Simpson** joined CBC'S *Hockey Night in Canada* as an analyst in 2007, bringing experience as an NHL forward, four years experience as an NHL coach, and more than 10 years of experience as an NHL broadcaster to his role. A knowledgeable and seasoned analyst, Simpson began his broadcast career in 1996 at The Sports Network (TSN) following his retirement from the NHL the previous year. He made a name for himself in the United States working with FoxSportsNet for two years. Simpson made his way back to Canada, joining Rogers Sportsnet in Edmonton, where he spent five seasons working an analyst both in the br booth and in studio. S won two Stanley C Edmonton, in 19 and continues distinction Oiler to sc season (5

Tim Wharnsby is a senior writer with cbcsports.ca and is widely regarded as one of the top hockey journalists in the country, having covered the Toronto Maple Leafs, the NHL and junior hockey for *The Globe and Mail* and *The Toronto Sun*. Tim also worked for the NHL Players' Association. Toronto resident is a regu guest on HNIC Radio SIRIUS with hock Jeff Marek an Tim also CBC's to pr

PHOTO CREDITS